What readers

The Inventor's Fortune Up For Grabs

"From a personal and professional point of view, I wasn't able to put it down. The humanistic aspects of the story carried the momentum of the entire book. *The Inventor's Fortune* stands as a testimony of the importance of helping clients identify, and then accurately document, the outcomes they desire for their family."

> James R. Graham
> Principal
> Greenberg|Graham Advisors LLC

"I found it to be a well-written, entertaining and fascinating story. I particularly liked how it was constructed: John's explanations of the legal issues helped ground Suzanne's more personal approach to the story. As a result, readers gain greater insight and context, which helps to better understand the complexity of the case."

> Richard Conroy
> Executive Director
> Essex (CT) Library Association

"This story is a more-than-readable demonstration that unlikely justice is sometimes achievable. All it requires is a willingness to challenge foregone conclusions. Of course, it's also helpful to apply a healthy measure of tenacity, teamwork, generosity, devotion to fairness, and an uncanny ability to promote cooperation and reason."

> Lew Treistman
> Acting Rhode Island State Medicaid Director, Retired

"I very much enjoyed reading *The Inventor's Fortune*. It's a well-written story with captivating twists and turns. As told by the authors, the story easily led me through the legal intricacies of the case and again reminded me of the vagaries of human nature."

> Robert S. Morton
> Ayrault House of Newport (RI)

"*The Inventor's Fortune* quickly places the reader dead center in the courthouse drama and in the lives of real people who are resolving complex issues. And it is done with a well-organized, easily read story. Written by two participants—a lawyer and a defendant—it offers as much education as it does entertainment. During my career, I was involved in much litigation, which makes this fine story all the more fun."

Maury S. Knowlton
Corporate Executive, Retired

"An intriguing story of a true legal case with many unanticipated and unique surprises!"

Marv Harshman
Former college basketball coach, Naismith Memorial Basketball Hall of Fame, 1985

*Bob + Amy,
Stay in good
health + keep
swimming!
♡
Hugs,
Sue :)
11-11-10*

THE INVENTOR'S
FORTUNE
Up for Grabs

The legacy of the expansion bracelet

Suzanne G. Beyer and John S. Pfarr

 BOOK PUBLISHERS NETWORK

Book Publishers Network
P.O. Box 2256
Bothell • WA • 98041
PH • 425-483-3040
www.bookpublishersnetwork.com

10 9 8 7 6 5 4 3 2 1

Printed in the United States of America

LCCN 2010934495
ISBN10 1-935359-53-3
ISBN13 978-1-935359-53-1

Back cover photo of John Pfarr: photo credit to Carl Keitmer

Prologue photo of Mr. and Mrs. Hadley with children: photo credit to Brown, Providence, RI

Chapter three photo of Alice Seeley with Jack and Stearns Gay: used with permission from Gustaf Ekman, Ekman's Studio, Bristol, VT

Chapter four photo of Cindy Gay and son Lane Williams: photo credit to Ginette Lemay, Wedding Photography, Lawrence, MA

Chapter seven photo of Lauren E. Jones, Esquire: photo credit to Brian McDonald

Editor: Lori Zue
Cover Designer: Laura Zugzda
Typographer: Stephanie Martindale

This book is dedicated to the memory of…

My late cousin, Cynthia "Cindy" Ruth Gay,
who always gave me sage advice and unwavering friendship.
Suzanne G. Beyer

And…

My late parents, John S. Pfarr and Susan E. Pfarr,
who collaborated to furnish me with a fabulous formal and informal
education and their unconditional love.
John S. Pfarr

CONTENTS

Authors' Note

This is a true story. This is how we remember the included events, which may not match the memories of all concerned. We compressed or estimated dialogue and correspondence to convey substance. When, despite our efforts, we could not verify the actual date of a reported event, we have estimated that date if it did not affect the veracity of the story.

WHO'S WHO

*in the legal battle to distribute Art Hadley's
fortune according to his wishes*

Hadley Family

Art Hadley—*inventor in 1913 of the expansion bracelet; died without
clear instructions as to who should inherit the fortune contained in
his two trusts in the event his children died without biological children*

Frances E. Hadley—*Art's wife and settlor of two additional trusts; the
three beneficiaries of her trusts were her two children, Thomas and
Sarah, from her marriage to Art Hadley, and the wife of her son
Thomas, Betty Hadley*

Thomas P. Hadley—*son of Art Hadley; one of two beneficiaries of his
father's trusts and a beneficiary of one of his mother's trusts; adopted
his wife's two daughters in 1976; no biological children of his own*

Betty Hadley—*married Thomas Hadley on March 8, 1962; Thomas
adopted her two daughters*

Sarah "Sally" L. Hadley—*sister of Thomas and the only other beneficiary
of Art Hadley's trusts; died with no children*

Una Hadley Gay—*sister of Art Hadley and mother of Alice Hadley Gay, Stearns Gay and Jack Gay, and grandmother of the eleven Hadley heirs-at-law*

May Gay—*sister of Art Hadley; died with no children*

Case Participants

Adopted Daughters of Thomas P. Hadley—*represented by John M. Harpootian*

>
> Janet Hunt—*adopted by stepfather Thomas Hadley on March 11, 1976*
>
> Lucille Foster—*adopted by stepfather Thomas Hadley on March 11, 1976*

Hadley Heirs-at-law (other than Janet Hunt and Lucille Foster)—*All but two, Rev. Ronald Eliot Gay and Wylma Gay Cooley, of the eleven Hadley heirs-at-law, were represented by John S. Pfarr; Ron and Wylma were represented by David J. Strachman*

> *Children of Alice Hadley Gay:*
>
>> Suzanne G. Beyer—*co-author of this book*
>>
>> Robert S. Seeley
>
> *Children of John "Jack" A. Gay:*
>
>> Wylma Gay Cooley
>>
>> Sheila Gay Franklin
>>
>> Allyson Gay
>>
>> Rev. Ronald Eliot Gay
>>
>> Diana Gay Robertson
>>
>> Wendy Gay
>
> *Children of L. Stearns Gay:*

Cynthia Ruth Gay—*died on October 11, 2006; succeeded by Estate of Cynthia Ruth Gay, with Sarah Gay Dagher, executrix*

Stephen H. Gay

Nancy G. Miller

Heirs-at-Law of Frances E. Hadley (14)—*eight were represented by Arthur M. Read II and six were represented by Edmund C. Bennett*

Estate of Sarah L. Hadley, Marcia E. Hanrahan, executrix—*represented by Paul A. Brule and Scott O. Diamond*

Estate of Thomas P. Hadley—*represented by James A. Bigos*

Trustee of the Art Hadley and the Frances Hadley Trusts—*originally Fleet National Bank and, later, Bank of America, as a result of Fleet's merger with Bank of America; represented by HinckleyAllenSnyder LLP*

Attorneys

Edmund C. Bennett—*counsel for six heirs-at-law of Frances E. Hadley*

James A. Bigos—*counsel for the Estate of Thomas P. Hadley*

Leon C. Boghossian III—*counsel for the trustee, Bank of America*

Paul A. Brule—*counsel for the Estate of Sarah L. Hadley, including beneficiaries Cindy Gay and Marcia Hanrahan*

Scott O. Diamond—*co-counsel with Paul A. Brule*

Renee A. R. Evangelista—*guardian ad litem for Hadley heirs-at-law (other than Janet Hunt and Lucille Foster); determined the eleven Hadley heirs-at-law had no right to any of the money in Art Hadley's or Frances Hadley's trusts*

John M. Harpootian—*counsel for the two adopted daughters*

Lauren E. Jones—*co-counsel with John S. Pfarr; expert in Rhode Island Supreme Court practice*

John S. Pfarr—*counsel for nine of the eleven Hadley heirs-at-law descended from Alice Hadley Gay, Jack Gay and L. Stearns Gay; co-author of this book*

Arthur M. Read, II—*counsel for eight of the heirs-at-law of Frances E. Hadley*

David J. Strachman—*counsel for Ron Gay and Wylma Cooley*

Mark P. Welch—*guardian ad litem for the heirs-at-law of Frances E. Hadley; determined the fourteen heirs-at-law of Frances Hadley had no right to any of the money in Art Hadley's or Frances Hadley's trusts*

Judges and Mediators

United States Supreme Court

Associate Justice David H. Souter—*handled administrative aspects of Ron's and Wylma's petitions for certiorari to the United States Supreme Court; participated in an associate justices' committee deciding the disposition of their petitions*

Rhode Island Supreme Court

Chief Justice Frank J. Williams—*former Rhode Island Supreme Court Chief Justice who wrote the opinion in Ron and Wylma's case; was also the trial court judge in the Rhode Island Superior Court Tinney v. Tinney (1999) decision; recused himself when the Rhode Island Supreme Court reached its decision in Tinney v. Tinney (2002)*

Justice Paul A. Suttell—*participated in the decision in Ron and Wylma's appeal*

Justice Francis X. Flaherty—*participated in the decision in Ron and Wylma's appeal*

Justice Maureen McKenna Goldberg—*participated in the decision in Ron and Wylma's appeal*

Rhode Island Supreme Court Mediators:

Retired Rhode Island Supreme Court Justice Donald F. Shea—*court-appointed co-mediator with CJ (ret.) Weisberger who withdrew from the Hadley case, and retired from the Supreme Court's mediation panel after the first mediation session on November 17, 2005*

Retired Rhode Island Supreme Court Chief Justice Joseph R. Weisberger (known as CJ (ret.) Weisberger)—*court-appointed co-mediator who continued as the sole mediator after the retirement of Justice (ret.) Donald F. Shea; helped broker the settlement of the Hadley case*

Superior Court (Trial Court) Justices:

Associate Justice Michael A. Silverstein—*original trial judge in the Hadley case who appointed Rhode Island Attorney Renee A. R. Evangelista of the Providence, Rhode Island law firm Edwards & Angell, LLP and Attorney Mark P. Welch as guardians ad litem to represent Art Hadley's heirs-at-law and Frances Hadley's heirs-at-law, respectively, as determined by Rhode Island statute. Also appointed Attorney James A. Bigos as counsel of the Estate of Thomas P. Hadley*

Associate Justice Susan E. McGuirl—*second trial judge in the Hadley case who ordered amendment of the trustee's Verified Petition for Construction of Trust and Order of Distribution to add the Art Hadley heirs-at-law (other than Janet Hunt and Lucille Foster) and the heirs-at-law of Frances Hadley as defendants so that they could argue their rights to any of the four Hadley trusts*

Associate Justice Daniel A. Procaccini—*third trial judge in the Hadley case who recused himself from the case on October 28, 2003 for reasons he never announced publicly*

Justice Allen P. Rubine—*fourth and final trial judge in the Hadley case who decided the case; his opinion satisfied none of the parties to the Hadley case fully, leading all of the parties to appeal his decision to the Rhode Island Supreme Court*

THE HADLEY FAMILY TREE

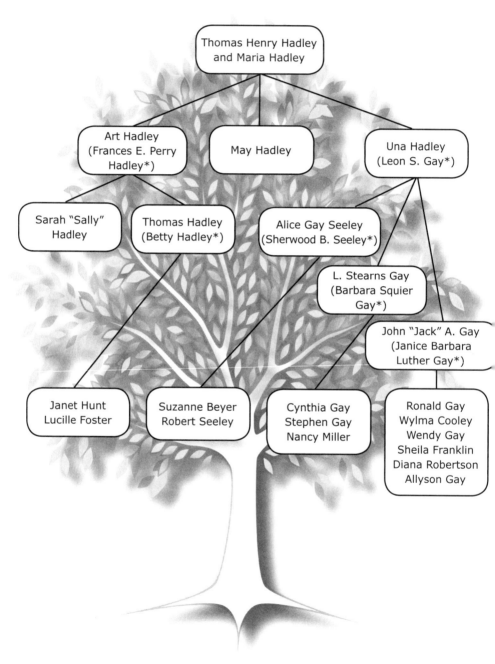

Thomas Henry Hadley
and Maria Hadley

Art Hadley
(Frances E. Perry
Hadley*)

May Hadley

Una Hadley
(Leon S. Gay*)

Sarah "Sally"
Hadley

Thomas Hadley
(Betty Hadley*)

Alice Gay Seeley
(Sherwood B. Seeley*)

L. Stearns Gay
(Barbara Squier
Gay*)

John "Jack" A. Gay
(Janice Barbara
Luther Gay*)

Janet Hunt
Lucille Foster

Suzanne Beyer
Robert Seeley

Cynthia Gay
Stephen Gay
Nancy Miller

Ronald Gay
Wylma Cooley
Wendy Gay
Sheila Franklin
Diana Robertson
Allyson Gay

* Spouse

Preface

Two Tales of the Same Story

With a mere click of the mouse, fate threw us together as active participants in a true story that has had profound consequences on each of our lives. The story revolves around the question of who inherits the $7 million fortune left by Rhode Island inventor and jewelry magnate Art Hadley, and his wife, Frances, and the quest to identify their rightful heirs. Our account describes a six-year journey—one replete with heartwarming human struggles, rollercoaster emotions, discord from surprising sources, intriguing legal maneuvers and gratifying results.

As co-authors, we're in a unique position to tell this story. Suzanne is Art's grandniece. She and several family members retained John, a Rhode Island attorney, to represent their interests.

Our story unfolded for each of us from very different perspectives. Although we considered writing separate books, each story would be incomplete without the other; the human drama and the legal proceedings were too tightly interwoven. Consequently, we've written the story of Art Hadley's fortune and its distribution from a dual perspective.

 John:

Suzanne and eight other descendants of Art Hadley engaged me to represent them in investigating whether they were entitled to any of the Art Hadley fortune. The story ended six years later, when Suzanne's group of nine settled the case for $1.8 million (roughly 90 percent of the maximum amount they were likely to inherit if the case had been decided by the courts).

What did we do to achieve that settlement? Why did my nine clients stick together despite enormous pressures to split apart? Why did the nine represented by me not receive 100 percent of what they were entitled to and why were two of Art's descendants (who represented themselves) left with nothing except expenses? This captivating tale answers those questions, and illustrates the significance of faith, commitment, family unity, spiritual guidance, the ups and downs and countless delays of the legal system, and the corruptive effect of greed and self-defeating arrogance.

Our account hinges on a set of facts and circumstances in a case that fell through the legal cracks. There was no clear winner or loser; there is no one who was right and no one who was wrong—simply a group of people fighting for what they believed was fair and in keeping with Great Uncle Art's wishes. Unfortunately, there was no governing law in Rhode Island that could provide a precedent to help decide this case. We were in uncharted territory.

That left the inventor's fortune up for grabs.

Who Would You Root for, Given One Unusual Fact?

In our story, you can take sides and root for your favorite characters as the tale twists and turns, although don't be surprised if you start rooting for the opposite team when new information comes to light. You won't be the only one! We do, however, promise you a happy ending; the good guys really do get to ride off into the sunset.

Background

Art Hadley, who died in 1941, divided his fortune between two trusts—a living trust and a testamentary trust.

Art left his fortune in these two trusts for the lifetime of his wife, Frances, and after her death, in trust for the lives of his two children, Thomas and Sarah. Art provided that at the deaths of Sarah and Thomas, these two trusts would end and the assets would be distributed to the children of Thomas and Sarah.

The terms of the two trusts were essentially the same, except in the event neither Thomas nor Sarah had children. This difference became critical because neither Thomas nor Sarah had any biological children.

Not only were the terms of the trusts different on this point, they also conflicted, which would cause very different outcomes under the two documents. While we will never know for sure, the difference was probably a drafting error by Art's attorney in the so-called boilerplate, or template, of the documents. Art Hadley signed both documents on the same day and must not have noticed the inconsistency.

The living trust (with over $2 million in assets)[1] clearly provided that the assets in that trust would be distributed among Suzanne, her brother and nine cousins if both Thomas and Sarah died without children.

The testamentary trust (with over $4 million in assets)[2], however, contained no directions as to what should happen if neither Thomas nor Sarah had children. This meant that the distribution was determined not by the terms of that trust, but rather by the Rhode Island legislature under Rhode Island's *intestacy* statute. That statute provided that the assets of this trust be distributed to Art's *heirs-at-law*. Who those people are would be determined at the time of his death, which was in 1941. This did not include any of Suzanne's family, but did include distant relatives of Frances, Art's wife.

Despite the enormous consequences stemming from the absence of one sentence in the testamentary trust, Art's beneficiaries under both the living trust and the testamentary trust joined together to confront a more pivotal issue: whether Thomas had truly died without children.

While Thomas had no biological children, in 1976 he did adopt his wife's two daughters from a previous marriage. This begs the question, would Great Uncle Art have intended his fortune go to those two adopted girls over his blood relatives? Most of us would probably resolve that issue in favor of the adopted daughters; after all, doesn't that reflect the values of our modern society, to not discriminate against children brought into a family by adoption rather than by birth?

Not only does that reflect our values, as observers, but those of Suzanne's family as well. In fact, nine of the eleven Hadley heirs-at-law (excluding the two who eventually represented themselves) agreed, without debate, that this would be the proper solution, were it not for one or two unique details about the adoption.

Introduction: Who Would You Root for,
Given One Unusual Fact?

xxi

At the time Thomas adopted his wife Betty's children, he and Betty had been married twelve years. One of the daughters, Janet, was thirty-two years old, divorced and living in San Diego at the time. The other daughter, Lucille, was thirty-one, married and living in Leeds, England.

If Thomas were successful in making these adult adoptees his children for purposes of his father's estate—both the living trust and the testamentary trust—then the adult children would take Thomas' entire share of the family fortune, even over any biological children of his sister Sarah, had she had children. Family legend has it that clever Thomas knew what he was doing, and that this is the very reason Thomas adopted these women.

So, to which group should the Hadley fortune be distributed? The two women adopted by Thomas or Art's blood relatives?

That is what the Rhode Island courts needed to decide, and what this book is about.

THE INVENTION THAT BUILT ART HADLEY'S FORTUNE

*Suzanne:*

When I opened my mother's jewelry box shortly after her death in 1982, I found a pretty expansion bracelet. Each link shined with a gold-plated surface; the links connected to a mechanism that allowed the bracelet to stretch and slide smoothly over my hand. Since it fit my wrist perfectly, and also suited my simple jewelry taste, I claimed it as mine.

"That expansion bracelet was invented by your Great Uncle Artie," Dad commented as he watched me slip it on my wrist.

I wore the bracelet every day for the next fifteen years. My grandmother had given it to my mother, and I felt closer to both of them when I wore it. Great Uncle Art Hadley was my grandmother's brother. I knew he was of British stock, born in South Africa in the 1880s. When Art was three years old, he and his sisters, Una and May, immigrated to America with their parents, Thomas and Maria, and settled in Providence, Rhode Island in 1888.

Art was lucky to have landed in Rhode Island, the heart of America's jewelry industry. He was smart and industrious. He attended Technical High School, worked as a toolmaker, then founded his own jewelry company—the Hadley Jewelry Company—where, in 1913, he created the first expansion bracelet, at the age of twenty-eight.

According to family gossip, Great Uncle Art liked beautiful women, sports cars and liquor. One story recounts that, after an overnight stay at my grandmother's Cavendish, Vermont home, Art recruited my Uncle Stearns to drive him to Montreal, Canada in his Auburn "Boat Tail" Speedster (the Ferrari of American cars in its day). The Montreal trip included smuggling a trunk load of bootleg booze into the U.S. during Prohibition. These stories of my colorful, creative Great Uncle Art sharply contrasted with my experience of the prim and proper British essence of my Grandmother Una, Art's sister.

As much as I enjoyed hearing those stories about him, what was most interesting to me was his invention of the expansion bracelet. The inscription on the inside of one of the bracelet's links reads *February 11, 1913*.

I knew only bits and pieces of his life and his work, but I wanted to know more. It was time to investigate.

While surfing the Internet, I discovered the nearby University of Washington's Engineering Library contained a complete set of the Official Gazette of the U.S. Patent Office. How lucky is that, I thought. I would be able to see for myself if my great uncle was listed in these impressive directories. On a rainy Sunday morning, I drove forty-five minutes to the school campus and waited on the steps of the library for it to open.

Once inside, I felt like I had entered a candy shop when I saw shelves of books containing our nation's patents. I was ready to explore.

I opened the *Official Gazette of the U.S. Patent Office* book to "H" and there it was: The Hadley Jewelry Company! In the document's first paragraph, I discovered the expansion bracelet invention was a collaboration between Great Uncle Art and his co-worker, Charles P. Kuehner. They had patented the bracelet on February 11, 1913, the same date indicated on the bracelet's inscription. An incredible find for me!

It was hard to grasp what I had just read, but proof lay right in front of me. My great uncle truly was a great inventor. My dad wore an expansion watchband. I had seen expansion watchbands and bracelets in jewelry stores. They appeared everywhere. I had discovered gold!

With photocopies of that patent in hand, I next contacted the Providence (Rhode Island) Public Library. A helpful librarian mailed me a copy of Art's obituary from *The Providence Journal*, dated May 28, 1941. Family history I'd only heard about now leaped off the printed page!

The obituary revealed Art had remained a British subject his whole life. He fought in the First World War in Mesopotamia, and afterward started an optical manufacturing company in England. He founded the Hadley Jewelry Company in 1905 and was its president until he retired in 1937. Members of Britain's upper echelon befriended him, and Great Uncle Art was a close friend of Ernest Bevin, England's Minister of Labor and National Service. Until his retirement, Art divided his time between England and the U.S. and between his two companies.

When I looked into what became of the Hadley Jewelry Company following Art's death, I discovered that Art's wife, Frances, had sold the company to Elgin National Watch Company. Bertram Kalisher subsequently purchased the Hadley Watchband portion from Elgin. I researched Kalisher, and could hardly believe when I found contact information for him. Mr. Kalisher is the editor of *Chronos Magazine*, founder and executive director of the American Watch Guild, and co-publisher and executive editor of *Watch and Clock Review*. Since there were no family members I could ask about Great Uncle Art, Bertram Kalisher would be my one and only opportunity to find out about my relative. I desperately wanted to email him, but the only contact I could find was a telephone number.

I nervously dialed his number, a list of questions scribbled on a scratch pad at hand. I just prayed he would know something about Art and that my questions would not be intrusive.

I began hesitantly, "Hello, Mr. Kalisher, this is Suzanne Beyer. I am the greatniece of Art Hadley."

Mr. Kalisher was delighted to hear from me and excited to tell me everything he knew about Great Uncle Art.

"Art Hadley was very clever mechanically. He ran a good business, and was a pioneer in his field." He added, "Everything Art made was dignified and in good taste. His products and business showed an artistic and orderly mind."

Mr. Kalisher explained the expansion bracelet became the forerunner of the expansion wristwatch band. Before WWI, women wore wristwatches affixed to a black ribbon supplied by Hadley Jewelry Company. Ribbons fell out of fashion in the '30s, and were replaced with the new expansion bracelets.

He described men serving in the armed forces during WWI who needed a watch they could wear on their wrist. Pocket watches were impractical because the face frequently broke when a soldier jumped into a foxhole. By the end of 1918, men often wore wristwatches. The expansion wristband grew even more popular in the '20s and '30s.

I took notes the entire time he talked, but I couldn't write fast enough. I hoped the bits of valuable information I hadn't written down would remain in my head long enough to get them on paper when we finished talking. After thanking Mr. Kalisher and saying our goodbyes, I raced to my computer to capture all the details swimming around in my brain.

This research proved a big deal for me. It tied history to the present day and, most importantly, to my own life. I was fascinated to learn the origin and importance of the expansion bracelet made by my very own great uncle! I couldn't believe I had just spoken with someone so closely connected to the Hadley name and the expansion bracelet invention.

Thomas Henry
Hadley and wife
Maria with children,
Art, Una (Suzanne's
grandmother) and May,
of Providence, Rhode
Island; April 12, 1890

May, Una and the inventor, Art Hadley; 1904

Thomas Henry Hadley and daughter Una at 269 Doyle Avenue, Providence, Rhode Island; circa 1905

May, Art and Una Hadley; circa 1905

Great Uncle Art Hadley holding Suzanne's mother, Alice Hadley Gay; September 1910

Glimmerstone, home of Suzanne's grandparents, Una and Leon Gay; Cavendish, Vermont

Una Hadley Gay serving proper afternoon tea at Glimmerstone, her Cavendish, Vermont home; circa 1945

Family gathering at Glimmerstone; Cavendish, Vermont; circa 1949
Pictured: Una Hadley Gay, Suzanne, Sherwood Seeley (Suzanne's father), Barbara Gay (wife of Stearns Gay), Leon S. Gay, Alice Hadley Gay Seeley and Robert Seeley (Suzanne's brother)

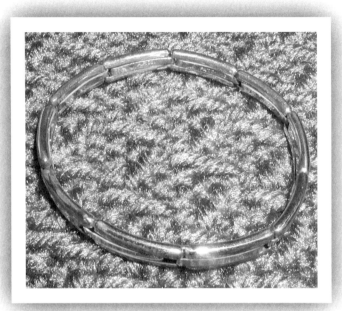

The original expansion bracelet invented by Art Hadley, patented
February 11, 1913

Bertram Kalisher (left)
and Robert Seeley
(Suzanne's brother)
meet at a New York
summer jewelry
tradeshow;
July 26, 2010

Chapter One

The Envelope

Suzanne:

You have been determined to be an heir-at-law of Arthur Hadley... stated the letter I received in January 2003. The author of the letter introduced herself as Renee Evangelista, a partner in the Providence, Rhode Island law firm of Edwards & Angell, LLP. She had been appointed by the court as the guardian ad litem to represent Art Hadley's heirs-at-law.

I was as excited as a child on Christmas morning when I read the letter, fully expecting to find a jackpot at the end of a rainbow. I could only imagine the big bucks my Great Uncle Art Hadley had accumulated from his Rhode Island jewelry company and his optical plant in England. His children had died, and now it was time to distribute the trusts' property to his family.

"We're going to be rich!" I thought. You can just imagine my shock, then, when I read the next sentence.

At this time, we believe it is unlikely that you will be inheriting under the Hadley Trusts.

What?! My newly acquired wealth had ended so abruptly?

In February, Renee Evangelista sent me, my brother and nine cousins a second letter, enclosing a detailed report of her findings. The letter ended with her opinion, "…[M]y analysis of the trusts in question concludes that the heirs-at-law of Arthur Hadley do not appear to inherit according to the terms of the Trusts and Rhode Island law."

She continued, "Please acknowledge that you have received and read the enclosed guardian ad litem report and consent to the court acting on this matter by signing the enclosed Acknowledgment…Please feel free to obtain your own attorney to review my report or if you have any questions about my analysis."

I was floored. Even the attorney appointed to represent our interest feels we have no case? Was she not going to fight for Art Hadley's heirs-at-law at all? Why did she even bother sending me that first letter? At this point, I needed to know my cousins' and brother's reactions to Attorney Evangelista's February letter and report—a letter which began on such a positive note, then ended so pessimistically, and her request for us to sign our lives away upon reading her report.

Emailing or telephoning my favorite cousin, Cindy Gay, was always a highlight for me. Cindy was ten years older than I, and overflowed with sound advice based on her gut intuition, book smarts and life experiences. She was the wise owl of the family.

Cindy questioned the legal document sent by Attorney Evangelista, and felt we, as blood relatives of Art Hadley, should be entitled to some of his estate. We had no idea how much money was in our great uncle's trusts, but Cindy's first guess was around $700,000. I initially thought, "That's a lot," but when I reflected on his genius, I just knew we were talking much, much more.

Cindy wrote me the following email on March 4, 2003: "The more I think about this hiring of a lawyer, the more I think we should. Why go down without a fight! I'm in. This will have to be done ASAP, 'cause the lawyer would have to get the trusts to read; go nutso reading them; look up cases that would help our case; write the brief. We need a good estate lawyer. Get a hold of our other cousins. See what Cousin Wendy says…how soon can she reach her siblings to tell them NOT to sign the acknowledgment. Let's Go for the Maybe Gold!"

I didn't waste any time looking for an attorney. At Cindy's suggestion, I found the online version of the respected Martindale-Hubbell® lawyer directory, searched for "Rhode Island Trust and Estate Lawyers," and randomly clicked the mouse on . . . John S. Pfarr.

 *John:*

One of Suzanne's cousins contacted me about this case. Once I had the opportunity to review Attorney Renee Evangelista's draft report and read Art Hadley's estate planning documents and relevant Rhode Island cases, I found it to be a fascinating and complex case; it had all the elements of a fabulous law school examination question. I quickly saw that every one of the parties had a valid and meritorious argument for their respective positions. There was no "right answer" in this case. Also, I did not believe Rhode Island would leave unresolved what appeared to be a direct clash on an important public policy issue between the Rhode Island legislature and the Rhode Island Supreme Court.

Had I not realized this at the outset, I would never have agreed to take a case with such poor prospects. That would have been the biggest mistake of my career!

Given Renee's grim prognosis for this case, by the time the case was over, by almost anyone's measure, we won! Still, were I a justice of the Rhode Island Supreme Court deciding this case, to this day I do not know how I would have voted. That's how complex and difficult this case was.

After finding and reading my profile in the Martindale-Hubbell® directory, Suzanne circulated my name and background among the others. She and Cindy decided their cousin, Wendy Gay of Gypsum, Colorado, was the appropriate person to contact me.

Wendy called, introduced herself and explained she was calling on behalf of herself, her siblings and her cousins to seek a second opinion from that of Attorney Evangelista. Wendy explained the little bit she understood about the case, primarily based upon the same letters and reports received by Suzanne from Attorney Evangelista. Knowing Renee's fine reputation as an attorney, I doubted I would find any basis for disagreement with her research and conclusion, but agreed to review Renee's initial letters and her draft report that had not yet been submitted to the court. Thinking this was probably a waste of Wendy's money, I set a nominal fee for reviewing their case.

CHAPTER TWO

SEEK A SECOND OPINION

*Suzanne:*

Cousin Cindy and I felt Cousin Wendy was the perfect family member to establish an initial relationship with Attorney John Pfarr. Wendy, personable and extroverted, was one of my Uncle Jack's six children. Wendy would ask Mr. Pfarr about his fees and report back to the rest of us.

We all wondered what it would cost for a lawyer to review the legal documents. My brother Robert said, "I'm guessing $3,000."

This became a cause for concern to a few of the cousins. Some could afford their portion of a fee that high, but others could not. I offered to help our cousin Cindy, who could barely get by financially.

We were all relieved that Robert's guess proved wrong. After receiving Art Hadley's estate planning documents and the guardian ad litem's report from Wendy, John Pfarr set a fee of $750 to give a second opinion.

Wendy's friend and later her husband, John Curran, dug into his pockets and advanced the $750 to John Pfarr on March 14, 2003, fully trusting that Wendy's siblings and cousins would reimburse him. I was impressed at John's kindness and trusting nature and sent my portion to him immediately.

A letter from Wendy to the rest of us said, "Due to these times, when everybody says, 'I'm so happy to sue you,' instead of 'I'm so happy to see you,' I felt that it is most important to send a copy of the letter and cashier's check that was sent to John Pfarr, who is most accommodating to assist us in our quest to understand all of the fancy lawyer talk that we have received in this matter."

Wendy finished her letter on an upbeat, welcoming note. "Perhaps it is time for us all to introduce ourselves and trade family stories that will help us to know one another…to me, that sounds like a fun idea."

I appreciated Wendy's thoughts and also liked the way Wendy communicated with Mr. Pfarr by exchanging well-written, polite and to-the-point letters. She sent copies of every piece of correspondence to us, including John's report on his opinion of our case.

Wendy, impressed with John's timely responses, usually ended her letters with, "Once again John, we thank you for all your help with the trusts and for taking us on as you did at the last minute. It has been a pleasure speaking with you and doing business."

Although we spoke of our Great Uncle Art Hadley's trusts, Wendy became philosophical and emotional when she looked up a different meaning to the word *trust*.

"One of the definitions of trust as a noun is 'the condition and resulting obligation of having confidence placed in one.' As a verb, it means 'to rely or depend on: have confidence.'" Wendy added her own thoughts to the definitions she shared, "I want all of you to know that I do appreciate my position with you in regards to dealing with those involved with the legal side of the trusts. It has been and will continue to be an honor. Through all of this, we have had to trust one another to carry out this mission, even though we really don't know one another."

Wendy believed this case would unite us into a solid group joining forces for one common cause. I could see that the family benefits

Wendy Gay and future husband, John Curran, on vacation at
Mt. Rushmore; September 2002

would be immense. Should John Pfarr proceed with our case, an extra bonus would be getting to know cousins I'd never met.

 John:

After obtaining a formal, signed engagement letter from Wendy, I began my analysis of this case by reading both the Art Hadley and the Frances Hadley estate planning documents, Attorney Evangelista's draft report, the Rhode Island cases cited in her report, a few other cases I found in the law library and by discussing the case several times with Renee. While I initially agreed with Renee that a recently decided Rhode Island Supreme Court case blocked any claim to this fortune by Wendy, her siblings and cousins, I intuitively felt this result should not be the law in Rhode Island. I urged Renee to amend the recommendation portion of her report to the court to the effect that "the Art Hadley heirs-at-law deserve to have their day in court to argue for a change in the law."

Renee agreed to make this change, which meant Wendy and her family were named as defendants in the case, giving them standing to challenge what Renee and everyone else expected would happen: the bulk of the Hadley fortune would pass to the adult-adopted daughters of Thomas Hadley. Persuading Renee to make this change was, perhaps, the first of the two most significant contributions I made to this case.

What bothered me, as I explained to Renee, was our belief that Thomas Hadley purposefully adopted the adult daughters of his wife for no other reason than to make them heirs of his father's fortune. He was already twelve years into his marriage to Betty when he adopted her daughters. The girls were in their thirties at the time they were adopted. One was married and the other married and subsequently divorced. Neither lived anywhere close to Thomas and his wife at the time of the adoption; one lived in California and one lived in England.

It was highly unlikely that Thomas would ever have children of his own. It was also pretty obvious that his sister, Sarah, was not going to have children either. If Thomas could successfully get the bulk of his father's fortune into the hands of his wife's daughters, then his wife would most likely be set for life.

The Rhode Island legislature, however, had already contemplated and then rejected such a strategy. In 1956 the Rhode Island legislature enacted a statute which states: an adoptee over the age of eighteen when adopted can not inherit from an ancestor of the adoptive parent under a will or other *written* document if the ancestor died before the adoption.[3] The facts of the Hadley case met all of the criteria to bar these women from inheriting as children of Thomas, as Art Hadley used that term in his two trusts.

Art Hadley died in 1941; the adoption occurred in 1976. These daughters of Thomas' wife had not even been born when Art Hadley died. We were interpreting two *written* documents—the Art Hadley Living Trust and the Art Hadley Testamentary Trust. Accordingly, under express Rhode Island statutory law, the adopted daughters, as adult adoptees, "lose" and the Art Hadley heirs-at-law "win."

Under the law, however, things are never as simple as they appear.

The Rhode Island legislature clearly disqualified Thomas' adult-adopted daughters from receiving anything under either of Art's trusts; accordingly, in the eyes of the law, both of Art's children died without children. That left the question whether Art gave any further instructions to cover this situation.

Art's living trust did; he simply directed the property in that trust be distributed to those persons who would inherit from him under the intestacy laws of Rhode Island in effect at the time of Sarah's death, January 3, 2002.[4] Were it not for a development occurring four months later, this clearly would have been Suzanne, her brother and her nine cousins.

By contrast, Art's testamentary trust failed to provide for this situation at all. The legal term for this is a "failure of trust." Rhode Island law states that in the event of a failure of trust, the property should be distributed to those persons who were Art's heirs-at-law on May 27, 1941, the date of Art's death.

Since Art's heirs-at-law under the testamentary trust were to be determined as of May 27, 1941, as opposed to January 3, 2002 per his living trust, this produced a totally different group of people than the living trust. This testamentary trust group did not include Suzanne, her brother or her nine cousins, but included heirs of Frances Hadley, Art's wife. In my professional opinion, Art would never have knowingly left his fortune to two totally different groups of people in this haphazard way.

Four months after Sarah Hadley's death, the Rhode Island Supreme Court issued its decision in *Tinney v. Tinney*,[5] a case that interpreted the meaning of the phrase, "those persons who would inherit from me under the laws of Rhode Island."

The *Tinney* case involved one of the famous Newport, Rhode Island mansions, Belcourt Castle. The matriarch of the family, Ruth Tinney, had one biological son. When she was eighty-four years old, she created something of a scandal when she adopted a thirty-eight-year-old man who provided maintenance work on Belcourt Castle, and had become practically part of the family. Mrs. Tinney died without a will or any other estate planning instructions. Therefore, her estate was slated to pass to those persons specified by Rhode Island's intestacy statute, irrespective of Mrs. Tinney's actual intent.

The adopted son claimed a share of Mrs. Tinney's estate equal to that of her biological son. The judge hearing the case agreed with the adult-adopted son, splitting Mrs. Tinney's entire estate equally between her two sons.

In May 2002, the Rhode Island Supreme Court affirmed the judge's decision and agreed that the adult-adopted son had equal status with the biological son. In its written opinion, the Rhode Island Supreme Court stated: "An adopted child is a 'child' of the adoptive parent irrespective of the age when adopted."

If this ruling applied to the Hadley case, as Attorney Evangelista and counsel for the adopted daughters and the trustee contended, then the adopted daughters would inherit most of Art Hadley's fortune, despite the fact that they were barred from inheriting anything by another Rhode Island statute.

This struck me as a bizarre result, because the two cases were very different. In *Tinney*, the supreme court's decision made sense. If a woman's relationship with someone is such that she adopts that person, isn't it reasonable she would want the adopted child to share with her other child any inheritance she left?

Tinney was a "direct" inheritance, from parent to child. The Hadley case was an "indirect" inheritance, where the inheritance passes from parent to child, who then adopts a third person unknown to the parent, attempting to make that third person a legal heir of the parent. If Thomas Hadley were successful in making his wife's daughters into the status of heirs-at-law of Art Hadley under Rhode Island's intestacy statute, then the Rhode Island legislature's attempt to limit this strategy would be clearly frustrated.

This dichotomy is what first attracted me to this case. I saw what I believed to be a significant inconsistency under Rhode Island law, and I wanted to see Suzanne and her family have an opportunity to argue for consistency between Rhode Island statutes and its supreme court's decision.

As I mentioned, Attorney Evangelista adopted my recommendation and amended her report to the court, advising the court that the Art Hadley defendants had one or more theories under which they could prevail; she recommended, therefore, that Bank of America's[6] request to the court for distribution instructions be amended to add the Art Hadley Heirs as defendants so they could have their day in court. Bank of America was the trustee of all of the Hadley Trusts—the two of Art's and the two created by Art's wife, Frances Hadley. The court accepted her recommendation, ordering the trustee's request for instructions amended to add the Art Hadley Heirs as defendants.[7]

The new defendants then went about finding legal counsel to represent them in arguing their respective positions. Since I did not accept contingent-fee cases, the form of legal engagement Suzanne and her family would require, I thought this would end my involvement with this case. I was, at least, satisfied I had won for them an opportunity to argue for consistency in Rhode Island law.

CHAPTER THREE

WE HAVE A LAWYER!

*Suzanne:*

Wendy telephoned me one day in July 2003 and, unable to contain her excitement, blurted out, "Guess who's coming to visit me?"

John Pfarr had scheduled a visit. Wendy couldn't wait to meet him: the gentleman she'd only corresponded with through letters until now, the lawyer who was found by one click of a mouse, and the friend he would become to our family.

Wendy was a self-declared tomboy, and lived on a ranch in Colorado. John's son lived in the same state, so on a visit westward to visit his son, John stopped by to meet Wendy. She was sold on him the first time they met.

"He's such a kind man," she said over and over, and added, "He's so interested in everything, including our horses and goats. We visited a long time! He didn't want to leave."

Wendy and her siblings Ron, Wylma, Sheila, Diana and Allyson grew up on a farm in Idaho raising horses and riding in rodeos. I never met these cousins, since the rest of us grew up on the east coast. Their father, my Uncle Jack, split from east coast tradition and moved his family westward when his firstborn, Ron, was a baby. This case was our first introduction to one another, via telephone and email communications.

After the court officially included us in the case, we asked John to represent us. He declined, stating that he did not accept contingent-fee cases. Wendy's sister, Sheila, also phoned John late in July 2003 to make a connection with him and discuss his handling of our case. Our family history intrigued him, but he initially felt we had very little chance of inheriting anything. He admitted being attracted to the case because of the challenge it represented, but he reiterated that he lacked the experience and expertise to represent multiple clients on a contingent-fee basis and, therefore, must decline.

In a late July 2003 email, John stunned all of us. "Our firm will represent you on a contingent-fee basis in an attempt to obtain a distribution for you from one or more of the trusts of Frances and/or Art Hadley."

I loved this idea. We wouldn't have to pay lawyer fees, but John would take a share of the trust distribution if we won or settled the case. If we lost, John would be out of luck, having worked for free, with us paying only his out-of-pocket expenses. This was a huge gamble on his part.

John had an impressive resume. He was a Harvard graduate, received his Juris Doctor *cum laude* from the University of Michigan Law School, had a successful trust and estate practice and was praised in *Worth* magazine as "one of the top 100 attorneys in the nation." With him representing us, how could we go wrong?

As soon as John accepted our case, we carried out his first request: appoint a group spokesperson!

His clients were Cindy Gay, Steve Gay and Nancy Miller,[8] who are the children of my Uncle Stearns; Wendy Gay, Sheila Franklin, Diana Robertson and Allyson Gay, the children of my Uncle Jack; and my brother, Robert Seeley, and me, the children of Alice Hadley Gay. We chose our oldest cousin Cindy as group spokesperson, and referred to her as the "point person." She immediately created a family tree so John could acquaint himself with his clients.

Alice Hadley Gay Seeley and Jack and Stearns Gay;
Bristol, Vermont; 1952

We, the blood relatives of Art Hadley, were now officially known as the "Art Hadley heirs-at-law." However, John declined to represent two of my cousins, Ron Gay and Wylma Cooley, out of a concern that their interests might eventually conflict with those of the rest of us. He did, however, agree to collaborate with their attorney, David J. Strachman, so long as there was no conflict between their goals and ours.

Our mission was to win some of our great uncle's trust monies, so it wouldn't all fall into the hands of his son Thomas' two adopted daughters—Janet Hunt and Lucille Foster. My brother and I and our cousins have always referred to them as "the girls." It's not that we had anything against adopted children inheriting, but we questioned Thomas' motive in the adoption of his wife's daughters, since "the girls" were thirty-one and thirty-two years old when adopted.

We didn't have a problem with the girls receiving *some* of the trust monies, but considering the history of animosity between Sarah and

Thomas, and the fact that Sarah had no children, we concluded that Thomas adopted the adult women so they could receive the bulk of Art Hadley's inheritance. We wondered if Art Hadley would have approved of Thomas manufacturing two new legal heirs.

I also wondered what, if anything, they knew about Art Hadley. Did they know how and when he invented the expansion bracelet? Did they know anything of our family history?

The girls presented the initial obstacle to our family receiving any part of Art's trust funds. Later, however, we came to realize it wouldn't be the girls who stood in our way, but two of our own blood relatives—Ron Gay and Wylma Cooley.

 *John:*

Early one bright July day in 2003, I heard from Wendy again after many months. (I remember the day she called; it was the Monday after the Fourth of July weekend when NBA basketball star Kobe Bryant was arrested just down the road from Wendy's home. She and I briefly discussed the Bryant case.) She telephoned to say that her group was having trouble finding a suitable attorney willing to accept this case on a contingent-fee basis and asked me to reconsider my decision not to take this case.

While the challenge inherent in the case was still as seductive as ever, I felt I had no choice but to decline again. In principle, I had no objection to contingent-fee engagements; in reality, I simply had no experience with such arrangements or with managing a number of contingent-fee clients, and had doubts as to my time and ability to do so in this complex case. Throughout my career, I had charged a fee for my legal services. While I knew from colleagues that contingent-fee arrangements could be lucrative, I was completely unfamiliar with this system and just had no idea what I would be getting involved in.

For example, how would I go about setting a fair percentage as the contingent fee? What if all eleven of my potential clients called or wrote me every day to discuss the case? I had visions of my practice taken over by a group of demanding clients who would incur no financial obligation when they contacted me.

My concerns went beyond the issue of managing the case, however. A troublesome worry was that my potential clients would disagree among themselves, and I would find myself in the middle of a dispute—an irreconcilable conflict of interest—with no alternative but to withdraw from the case after investing countless hours in it. I was so concerned by these possible problem areas that I declined accepting a just cause I felt I might be able to win.

My phone rang when I was working one evening later that same month. Sheila Franklin, one of Suzanne's cousins, introduced herself and explained she was calling to ask me again to represent her group. She and I talked for an hour while I explained my reasons for feeling uncomfortable taking this case. I ended the call repeating that I could not represent them in this case.

After I hung up, however, I again thought long and hard about my decision. I knew how interesting and challenging this case was going to be and that realization stoked my competitive spirit—the one that roots for the underdog. While I considered the Art Hadley heirs' chances a long shot, I felt they deserved to be represented, but recognized they could not afford to pay attorney's fees. I knew I would follow the development of this case regardless of whether I was officially involved. I also knew I would contribute in any way possible, even if I were not compensated. Worse, I simply hated the idea of sitting on the sidelines, watching someone else botch what felt like *my* case.

This was a once-in-a-career opportunity and I wasn't quite ready to let it go, so I explored what I would need to do in order to accept the case.

I called Bernie Rethore, one of my Phoenix office law partners who regularly handles contingent-fee cases, soon after my telephone conversation with Sheila. I explained the legal issues involved, and my thoughts as to how I might win the case. I also shared my significant reservations about taking a contingent-fee case and my conflict-of-interest concerns.

Law partners Bernard "Bernie" M. Rethore (left) and co-author John S. Pfarr of Pfarr & Rethore, PC

Bernie just laughed. "John, this is the challenge you have been waiting for your entire career!" He encouraged me not to worry about the contingent-fee aspects of the case; he assured me that he and our other partner, Bill Graves, would support me through those issues. He sent me an example of a contingent-fee agreement he uses, which addressed many of my client-management concerns.

Ninety minutes after hanging up the phone with Sheila, I called her back, told her I had reconsidered my position and would take the case, but with several conditions. After going over the conditions with Sheila, she assured me that none of her siblings or cousins would have any objections to my conditions.

These conditions were:

1. The group had to agree upon a single spokesperson who would be the only person who could contact me without incurring an additional fee. While I would render written reports directly to all of my clients as developments occurred in the case, all individual responses and questions needed to be coordinated with the spokesperson, and then the consensus communicated to me by the spokesperson.

2. I reserved the right to charge an hourly rate to any individual client who would not communicate to me through the spokesperson. (While I did receive more than three hundred phone calls, emails and letters directly from my individual clients over the course of the litigation, I never exercised my right to charge an extra fee since this direct contact never became burdensome or out of control.)

3. There would be no private or confidential conversations between me and any individual client. Each of my clients had to authorize me to disclose to the entire group anything said or written to me. (A couple of my clients tested me on this early on, and became embarrassed when I advised all of my clients of information I had received from one of them; after a couple of months, no one tried to swear me to secrecy again.)

4. I chose not to represent two members of the eleven-person group—Ron Gay and his sister, Wylma Cooley. I had had at least one telephone conversation with Ron prior to my conversation with Sheila; Ron and several of his sisters had told me that Wylma would follow whatever decisions Ron made. I liked Ron, a minister of an Evangelical church in Wisconsin. He was polite, articulate and extremely bright. My instincts, however, told me that he might not be receptive to or follow legal advice. He insistently explained to me his theory of the case, how it

was to be approached, and how, based upon a Judeo-Christian definition of *family*, the courts would necessarily decide the case in favor of the Art Hadley Heirs. In my judgment, his and Wylma's goals were incompatible with the goals of the other nine; I felt quite certain that, if I agreed to represent these two, I would soon find myself in an impossible conflict between Ron and Wylma and the remaining nine siblings and cousins. As the case developed, I learned that never before in my entire thirty-five-year legal career had my gut instincts served me so well.

All nine members of the group accepted my conditions, and appointed Cindy Gay as the point person to represent the group in communications with me. I thought of my clients as the "Mighty Nine." Cindy turned out to be an excellent choice and a genuine pleasure for me to work with.

In fact, Cindy became an inspiration and a reason why I fought so hard for this group. So many mornings I came into my office, opened my email and was greeted with something from Cindy on a garishly colored background, full of graphics and ending with her characteristic smiley face and the words, "We just wanted to let you know again how much we appreciate all you are doing for us."

CHAPTER FOUR

CINDY, OUR POINT PERSON

*Suzanne:*

Cindy knew our family history better than anyone. She had a lot of time to spend on this task, was well organized and kept good records. My brother, Robert, and I have always considered Cindy to be the family's CEO of Smarts and Common Sense, and had full confidence she'd perform her duties well.

I recall meeting Cindy for the first time when I was ten while visiting Princeton University where her fiancé went to college. Her funny, vivacious personality and her Liz Taylor-like face and figure lit up the room. I wanted to be just like her when I grew up. Cindy held an English degree from the University of Vermont and was an accomplished stage actress in several theater groups, where she performed leading roles in plays such as *The Subject Was Roses* and *On Golden Pond*.

Simply put, she was my idol.

Now in her sixties, she worked for Whitman College in Walla Walla, Washington as their Summer Dance Lab coordinator, and had many artsy friends. Her two cocker spaniels and her picture-perfect rose gardens rounded out her loves.

John wanted to learn more from Cindy about the relationships among the Hadley family members. Cindy knew Great Uncle Art's daughter Sarah, or "Sally," and had visited her in her Providence home each year. Cindy described Sally as most gracious, bright and an accomplished pianist. The two were fond of each other and talked often.

Cindy wrote to me, "I told John how Sally and her brother, Tommy [Thomas Hadley], did not get along. He asked me if I knew the girls were adults when they were adopted. I responded, 'Are you kidding?' Sally had only mentioned that Tommy had married a lady named Betty and that she had two kids."

Cindy continued, "John asked me what I thought of the adoption of the girls as adults. I told him I honestly believed Tommy—smart as a whip and rather diabolical—knew exactly why to adopt at that age."

Cindy felt Tommy didn't like Sally, for whatever reasons. Sally had some mental health problems, had been institutionalized at one point, and was in and out of group therapy. Cindy believed this emotional instability may have resulted from Sally's fiancé's death as a Royal Air Force pilot shot down during the Battle of Britain. Following that heartbreak, Art took Sally on a trip to England, where she met another gentleman. Art didn't like or trust this man, and the young couple's possible union never stood a chance, which added to her emotional imbalance.

On one of her visits, Sally confided in Cindy that, in the event of her death, Cindy would receive an inheritance from her, but warned Cindy that Tommy was the controlling figure in her father's estate.

Cindy was devastated at the news of Sally's death in January 2002. She soon learned she was named in Sally's will as one of the beneficiaries of her estate, an estate that included a one-half interest in the two trusts established by her father and in one trust established by her mother.

Just over a year later, a friend of Cindy's mentioned she was having a mammogram, which reminded Cindy that this was the first year she had forgotten to get the routine test. She decided to make an appointment.

Cindy Gay with son, Lane Williams, walking down the aisle at her
daughter Sarah's wedding; 1988

In October 2003, Cindy's doctor delivered some devastating news. "You have breast cancer."

Cindy had had a gut feeling the news would be bad and wasn't shocked by the diagnosis. A woman just knows! To confirm his diagnosis, the doctor performed a biopsy in November 2003, followed immediately by a mastectomy. Cindy endured chemotherapy from January 2004 through July 2004.

 *John:*

Having agreed to represent Suzanne, her brother and nine cousins in the Hadley case, the first major step I took was to speak to the attorney for the two adopted daughters to see if there was any interest in discussing a settlement of the case. John Harpootian, their counsel, claimed that Rhode Island law was clear: his clients were the grandchildren of Art Hadley and, as such, the bulk of the Art Hadley fortune was legally theirs. Therefore, he had no incentive to discuss settlement.

I also spoke to Leon Boghossian, counsel for trustee Bank of America, to see if he would encourage Attorney Harpootian to have settlement discussions with me. He declined, saying that my clients had been included in this case on a technicality and that Rhode Island law was "settled law" (in favor of Thomas' adopted daughters). I made these two attempts to discuss settlement in September 2003. Within fifteen months, those attitudes had dramatically changed.

Six different parties, or classes of parties, participated in this case, including one institution, two estates and twenty-eight individuals:

Trustee Bank of America; represented by Attorney Leon C. Boghossian III

Adult-adopted daughters Janet Hunt and Lucille Foster; represented by Attorney John M. Harpootian

Fourteen heirs-at-law of Frances Hadley: one group represented by Attorney Arthur M. Read, II, and another group represented by Attorney Edmund C. Bennett

Eleven Art Hadley heirs-at-law: Ron Gay and Wylma Cooley were represented by Attorney David J. Strachman; I represented the balance

The Estate of Sarah L. Hadley, represented by Attorneys Paul A. Brule and Scott O. Diamond

The Estate of Thomas P. Hadley, represented by Attorney James A. Bigos

The trial judge assigned to hear this case had set February 1, 2004 as the deadline for filing of the initial legal briefs by the various parties. I spent approximately twenty-five hours in the Rhode Island Supreme Court Law Library during September, October and mid-November 2003 researching Rhode Island law. I was focused on finding legal precedent that contradicted the contention that the Rhode Island's decision in the *Tinney* case settled this matter in favor of the adult-adopted daughters. I found very little to work with, except some old case law that supported a couple of "Hail Mary" theories I had begun to develop.

A major obstacle for me was that I agreed with the *Tinney* decision; had I been a justice of the supreme court, I would have decided that case in exactly the same way the Rhode Island Supreme Court did.

Technically, however, *Tinney* did not apply to our case. The facts in *Tinney* were simple: (i) An eighty-four-year-old single woman adopted a thirty-eight-year-old man as her son; (ii) she had a biological son with her deceased husband; and (iii) she died without a will. The legal term for this is "dying *intestate*."

The Rhode Island intestacy statute mandates that, when a single person dies *intestate* and is survived by "children," the deceased person's estate is divided equally among the children. The only question before the Rhode Island Supreme Court in *Tinney*, therefore, was whether she had one child or two. Brushing aside as irrelevant the argument by the biological son that the adopted child was adopted as an adult, the Rhode Island Supreme Court decided that she had two children.

Whenever the Rhode Island Supreme Court makes a decision, that decision (referred to as its "holding") automatically becomes the law of Rhode Island.[9] The holding, however, is limited to the precise facts involved in that case. Any language in a court's opinion that goes beyond those facts is called *dicta*. *Dicta* might give a clue as to how a future court will decide when that court is presented with the same facts discussed in the *dicta*, but *dicta* establishes no law.

In the United States legal system, courts decide only actual, disputed cases, based upon the precise facts of that case. When advocates argue for the genuine interests of the parties involved in a suit, the court then has for its consideration all of the relevant facts and best arguments for the respective positions it needs before rendering a decision; hence, it is more likely to render a well-reasoned, well-considered opinion.

The reason why the Rhode Island Supreme Court's decision in *Tinney* was *dicta,* as it relates to the Hadley case, is that no one argued in *Tinney* why the court's holding should not apply to indirect inheritances. The courts of fourteen other states have looked at this issue and concluded that permitting adult-adopted persons to become an heir of other than the adoptive parent is fraught with potential for abuse. I felt our state supreme court deserved to hear the public policy arguments why it might not be wise to extend the *Tinney* holding to indirect inheritances.

Our task and opportunity was to make this argument, and persuade the Rhode Island Supreme Court that it should bar adult-adoptees from inheriting in an indirect inheritance situation. After all, we would be asking the Rhode Island Supreme Court only to make the same distinction that the Rhode Island legislature had made almost forty years earlier when it passed legislation excluding Thomas' adult-adopted daughters as "children" under Art's estate planning documents.

While it is true that Art Hadley had extensive estate planning documents, under the rules of legal construction, everyone involved in the case (including me, *initially*) was in agreement that Art Hadley's documents were incomplete and, therefore, he had died "partially intestate." This means that, while he had estate-planning documents, the instructions contained in his testamentary trust did not specify how to distribute his property in the event neither Thomas nor Sarah were survived by children. Under Rhode Island law, when existing estate planning documents fail to give complete instructions, the courts then look to the intestacy statutes to fill the gap.

By contrast, in his living trust, he did leave instructions for this eventuality by merely incorporating into his trust agreement the Rhode Island intestacy statute.

The Rhode Island legislature had already excluded the adult-adopted daughters as children of Thomas precisely because they had been adopted as adults after the death of Art Hadley. Therefore, for legal analysis purposes, neither Thomas nor Sarah was survived by children, as that term had been defined by the Rhode Island legislature.

That meant that the court must look at Art's alternative instruction—go to the Rhode Island intestacy laws to determine who inherits. If the supreme court intended the *Tinney* holding to include indirect inheritances as well as direct inheritances, then we were finished, and the irony of all ironies would have ensued: while the adult-adopted daughters were barred by Rhode Island statute from inheriting under the express terms of Art's estate planning documents, they nevertheless qualified as "children" under Rhode Island's intestacy statute, as interpreted by the Rhode Island Supreme Court in *Tinney*. I had no choice but to confront the *Tinney* case head on and attempt to get the Rhode Island Supreme Court to limit its holding only to circumstances involving a direct inheritance.

I sat down on December 12, 2003 and spent that day and the next writing the most favorable memorandum of law (which I refer to as the Hadley Heirs' Brief) I could come up with, based on my exhaustive research of Rhode Island law.

When I read the product of that weekend's work, I was depressed; I concluded that, despite my best arguments as to why the supreme court should limit *Tinney* to a direct inheritance, we would lose the case nonetheless. Clearly, the supreme court already had evidenced a predisposition that the age of adoption was irrelevant in deciding whether an adopted child was a "child," as reflected in its *Tinney* decision. What I had to say in that initial brief gave the supreme court insufficient reasons to overcome that predisposition when applying its rationale to an indirect inheritance.

Furthermore, Art's very own instructions in his living trust directed that his property be distributed to those persons who would inherit it under Rhode Island's intestacy statute. How was I to get beyond that clear instruction? Since the testamentary trust was silent on the subject, I had the same problem with this trust also, since Rhode Island law requires distribution in accordance with the very same intestacy statute.

The best argument I had to work with was that the court's holding in *Tinney*, if extended to an indirect inheritance, would conflict with the Rhode Island legislature's public policy decision that the term "children" used in a trust does not include adult-adoptees unknown to the person creating the trust.[10]

Still, I simply did not believe I had written a persuasive enough argument to cause the Rhode Island Supreme Court to limit its holding in *Tinney* only to the *Tinney* facts.

On December 15, I sent this initial brief to Attorney Strachman, the attorney for Ron Gay and Wylma Cooley. Since Ron and Wylma had the identical interest that my clients had, and no conflict of interest had yet arisen among them, I had agreed to collaborate with Attorney Strachman to write a single Hadley Heirs' Brief.

During the fall of 2003, Attorney Strachman was immersed in a case against the Palestine Liberation Organization (PLO). Accordingly, he and I agreed I would do the research for—and write the initial version of—our joint brief, which we would both edit, once the demands of his PLO case permitted. Since he was a highly experienced litigator, and I had little litigation experience, we agreed that he would also be responsible for all procedural matters.

I also sent the initial draft brief to a respected friend and colleague, Providence Attorney Lauren E. Jones, to request his comments. At that time and to this day, Lauren argued more cases before the Rhode Island Supreme Court than any other attorney, as well as being past president of the Rhode Island Bar Association. I valued Lauren's ability to predict the responses of the various supreme court justices to particular arguments and legal issues.

Lauren was much more optimistic than I about the prospects for my initial draft of the Hadley Heirs' Brief, giving it a 40 percent chance of persuading the Rhode Island Supreme Court to rule in our favor on the adult-adoption issue.

While I greatly appreciated his confidence, feedback and suggestions, the most significant outcome of his review of the brief was that he developed an intense interest in the case, particularly the challenges posed by presenting our side of the case. From that moment on, Lauren was a committed advocate for our side in this debate. His interest and encouragement brought needed energy to my efforts and, most significantly of all, led to his eventual involvement in the case itself.

By the time I had sent this initial brief to Dave Strachman and Lauren Jones, I had already decided to scrap my initial brief entirely and start that same day with a new brief.

Up to that point, I had limited my research to Rhode Island law. What the courts of other states have to say about a particular issue is not usually regarded as very persuasive authority to the local court; the Rhode Island Supreme Court, for example, is normally not particularly interested in what the Colorado Supreme Court has to say on an issue before the Rhode Island Supreme Court.

As I began to outline my ideas for a new brief that mid-December afternoon, a light bulb went on in my head, and I suddenly saw an entirely new theory as to how I could frame the issues in this case for the court. The most exciting aspect of my new theory was that it would not require the Rhode Island Supreme Court to overrule its *Tinney* decision. I cannot exaggerate how mystical this experience was; it seemed to come from somewhere outside of myself.

First, I realized that, in interpreting Art's instructions, his actual intent in giving those instructions was paramount. Although he incorporated Rhode Island's intestacy law, the court had an obligation to define what Art actually meant by that reference.

While I and each of the other advocates purported to articulate Art's intent in our respective briefs with the same conviction as if we had talked to him yesterday, the truth is that none of us, including any court looking at the issue, knew how Art would resolve this matter if we could have consulted him.

Therefore, my new approach included laying before the court the considerations Art most likely would think important in December 1940, when he last revised his instructions. After all, the word "adoption" usually automatically brings to mind a baby or a small child. How could he possibly have contemplated his son adopting two mature women with families of their own in order to make the women Art's grandchildren?

Did Art truly intend to give the Rhode Island legislature and the Rhode Island courts a blank check with their power to amend or interpret the intestacy statute? What if the Rhode Island legislature revised the intestacy statute to provide that an intestate's entire estate went to the State of Rhode Island? Is there any doubt that he would have objected to that?

Second, since the Rhode Island Supreme Court had never ruled on the precise facts of the Hadley case, and since there was no other Rhode Island statutory or judicial authority coming anywhere close to dealing with these facts, I wrote:

"This is a case of first impression that has significant policy and public interest implications to Rhode Island."

As ideas flowed and the structure of my new brief unfolded, I drove home the fact that many other states had dealt with this issue, finding abuse and frustration of decedents' intent by permitting adult-adoptees to inherit in indirect inheritances situations. I wanted the justices of the Rhode Island Supreme Court to realize they had an opportunity to learn from the experiences of these other states *before* deciding what Rhode Island law would be on this issue.

How did I know all of this? I didn't; I just made these assertions up out of thin air.

Cloistered in my office and writing, in effect, a fantasy brief, unconstrained by actual statutory or case law, I started fabricating cases with facts that supported my new theory of the case—that, by letting Thomas Hadley "bootstrap" his wife's adult children into becoming his father's grandchildren, the court would be opening up the proverbial Pandora's Box of abuses.

For example, one of the cases I made up was a decision by the supreme court of the State of X (the name of the state was to be filled in if and when I found such a case). In my fabricated case, I imagined a man as the beneficiary of a trust set up by his father. The trust provided that, at the beneficiary's death, the trust would terminate and the assets distributed to his children. If he had no children, then the assets would go to his sister's children. In my scenario, the man had no children. He hated his sister and especially her children. To prevent the assets from being distributed to his nieces and nephews at his death, he adopted his wife as his "child."

This little vignette may seem amusing, but the significance of the story is that I subsequently found an actual case with practically identical facts to my made-up case. This case came from my birth state, Kentucky.[11]

I have to confess to experiencing goose bumps when I discovered it. By this point in my involvement with the Art Hadley case, I was already experiencing a sense of somehow being led in all of my endeavors on behalf of my clients. I, a rational, pragmatic, conservative lawyer, felt driven to win this case on their behalf and bring about the result Art would have intended.

When I told Attorney Strachman about the Kentucky case and a couple of other helpful cases from that state that I had identified, he suggested I take on the enormous task of researching the law of the other forty-nine states to see if others had dealt with this situation, and if so, what decisions their respective supreme courts had reached, as well as what public policy considerations had these courts deemed important. I agreed to undertake this task since I knew how powerful our position would be if I could prove that a majority of our nation's states barred adult-adoptees from inheriting in indirect inheritance situations.

Yale Law School is about forty minutes from my home in Essex, Connecticut, and has a law library much more extensive than that of the Rhode Island Supreme Court. As a Connecticut attorney, I had unobstructed access to the entire collections of the library. By this time, it was mid-December 2003. Since this was the December examination period at Yale Law School, the library was open 24/7. I took advantage of this and pulled a couple of all-nighters, researching and then reading case after case at the library. My fifty-state survey revealed that twenty-two states had cases dealing with the rights of an adult-adopted person to inherit as a child of the adoptive parent in cases where the inheritance was indirect. Of those twenty-two states, fourteen prohibited adult-adoptees from inheriting indirectly from a person other than the adoptive parent. Texas's individual courts were split over the issue. My research led to the creation of a document surveying and analyzing all of these cases in the twenty-two states that had dealt with the issue.

I finished my fifty-state research just before the law school closed for the holiday break. On December 23, 2003, I started drafting my new Hadley Heirs' Brief, a dramatically different brief than the initial one I had discarded. Armed this time, however, with substantial judicial authority to support my new theory (albeit from states other than Rhode Island), the words just flowed onto the paper.

In memorandum form, I also noted the results of my fifty-state survey, which would serve as legal analysis for use by the court, and that we would attach as an exhibit to our final brief. I then sent a copy of the new brief and an outline for the fifty-state memorandum to Attorneys Strachman and Jones.

Dave Strachman is an excellent writer and talented attorney. During January 2004, we scheduled four day-long editing sessions, writing and rewriting this new brief several times, sometimes completing two drafts in a single day. Dave's suggestions as to how to make our arguments cleaner, clearer and crisper materially improved our brief. By the time we submitted the Hadley Heirs' Brief to the court in early February 2004, I was convinced that we would win—maybe not before the trial judge, but once we argued the case before the Rhode Island Supreme Court.

Procedurally, before we could bring the matter to the Rhode Island Supreme Court, the lower trial court had to make a decision on the issues first. Justice Allen P. Rubine, by then the fourth trial court judge assigned to this case, had only recently been appointed to the bench; we expected him to be conservative, play it safe and merely follow the *dicta* contained in *Tinney*, deciding against us on the most critical adult-adoption issue. If that happened, we planned to appeal to the Rhode Island Supreme Court. We also knew that, should the trial judge decide in our favor, the other side would then appeal that decision to the Rhode Island Supreme Court.

Consequently, we were not particularly concerned with how the trial judge decided; everyone knew that this case would ultimately be decided by the Rhode Island Supreme Court.

CHAPTER FIVE

FINALLY, A RAY OF HOPE

*Suzanne:*

I was excited for Cindy when I heard about Sally's will. Sally mentioned two people in her will; one was Marcia Hanrahan, Sally's friend and executrix, and the other was Cindy. It appeared Cindy would inherit a lot of money. Not only could she receive Sally's willed portion, but she would also remain with us heirs-at-law in our pursuit of a share of Art's trusts. This was the best scenario for Cindy, as she was in the poorest health of us all, with mounting bills and living on a poverty-level income. I couldn't have been happier for her.

In August of 2003, our two cousins, Ron and Wylma, found their own lawyer, David Strachman, with whom John would collaborate. Ron and Wylma strongly felt that only blood relatives were entitled to Art Hadley's trusts and that in no way should the adopted adult daughters of Art's son Thomas get anything. The rest of us—my brother, our cousins and I—felt much differently and would welcome sharing with the girls in case of a settlement.

Despite differences between Ron's and Wylma's thinking and that of the rest of us, John brought hope to us heirs-at-law with the announcement in late December 2004 of a possible settlement with highly favorable terms for us!

John's point was that none of the litigants created this minefield of a dilemma and said, "Art and his attorney created this situation. Reasonable minds can disagree as to what Art intended but the truth is that he was probably never asked the correct questions, so he never told us what he would want to happen under the circumstances we now have. This situation was never anticipated, in my opinion, which is why the documents are ambiguous."

John continued, "There are over thirty parties to this litigation. Any one of you, Ron or Wylma, or any of the multitudes of other parties, can scuttle a settlement. In fact, I expect that someone will do exactly that."

John's foreboding words were punctuated with a buzz that cousins Ron and Wylma didn't want to settle.

On January 21, 2005, distressing news came from Attorney Boghossian, counsel for the trustee. We received a copy of his letter addressed to Honorable Allen P. Rubine, Providence Superior Court, which said, in part, "Although it appeared for a moment that settlement of the Hadley Trusts would be reached, that was evidently only wishful thinking on our part. We all tried our very best to resolve this case, but with so many clients, it was impossible to satisfy everyone. Consequently, no settlement will be reached with the distribution of the Hadley Trusts."

My heart sank, but then I got angry over the thought of a failed settlement. I wondered, "Isn't settling the reasonable thing to do? You know, take the high road?" We had come so close, but Ron and Wylma declined the offer to settle. John, who had had concerns from the beginning, reluctantly terminated his collaboration with Attorney Strachman.

I desperately felt the need to appeal to Ron's and Wylma's giving nature and make a last-ditch effort to connect with them in hopes that at some point, they would change their minds.

My letter to Ron, dated January 30, 2005, with a copy to Wylma, began, "It's amazing that all of the cousins have a cause to unite after fifty years. At least, I think I was around ten when I met you, Ronnie, in Vermont. You were a cute baby, and the only little one in the family."

I told him about the history of our great uncle's expansion bracelet invention and also reminisced about his dad, my adored, fun-loving Uncle Jack. I talked about my memory of Jack babysitting my brother and me, taking us for a ride in a small airplane, flying over our grandparents' home in Cavendish, Vermont, and how we coasted down a mountain in his old car, laughing our heads off.

I then switched my focus to our elder cousin, Cindy, and wrote, "The past two years have been sad ones. Cindy had to retire because of poor health, diabetes and cancer, with resulting surgery and months of chemotherapy until last July. She lives in a small house on social security checks and food stamps, and struggles to stay afloat both financially and health wise. Although you'll never hear her complain!"

I continued, "We cousins had a sterling opportunity to settle in the Hadley Trust case…an opportunity which suddenly opened to Hope, when there initially was none, regarding gaining a portion of Art Hadley's trust. Not only would some of the trust help my family with two kids in college, but it would literally turn Cindy's life around. That secure feeling of being able to live the rest of her life in comfort, completely out of medical bill debt, would guarantee her a sense of peace."

My pleas to Ron and Wylma continued, presented in the common sense manner taught to me by my role model, Cindy.

The following week, I got a response. Ron was pleased to hear from me and mentioned how unusual it was to have cousins who had never met and who didn't know each other. I felt the same.

Ron thanked me for the history of the bracelet, and for my recalling fun times with his dad, my Uncle Jack. Ron explained that his dad did

Jack Gay; Staten Island; circa 1945

not fit into any molds of accepted proper behavior and perhaps that's why we kids liked him so much. He was a kid just like us.

Ron then wrote about the case and Hadley's trusts, noting that his decision to not join us in settling was unpopular with our group and also misunderstood. However, Ron said that he had studied Rhode Island law extensively, had made his choice not to settle and would stand by this choice. Ron's letter was thoughtful and well written and I was happy to have the opportunity to get to know him, even if it was only through a letter exchange.

John also emailed us the following opinion: "Unless both Ron and Wylma change their positions, we are going to have to wait for the court to act. The Judge had promised to be prompt if we failed to settle, so I hope he keeps his promise."

We then nervously awaited Judge Rubine's decision as to whom would inherit Great Uncle Art's fortune.

 *John:*

After the initial briefs were filed by the litigating parties to the suit,[12] each of the attorneys read each other's briefs.

The brief filed on behalf of Janet Hunt and Lucille Foster merely cited the *Tinney* case and stated:

> In *Tinney*, our supreme court was asked to determine whether a child adopted as an adult by an intestate decedent had the same right of inheritance as a natural born child or a child adopted as a minor. Our supreme court held that they do.

Attorney Harpootian, their counsel, added to his brief, "After marrying Betty on March 8, 1962, Thomas essentially became a father to Betty's daughters and, out of love and affection, adopted Janet and Lucille as adults on March 11, 1976," but he offered no evidence whatsoever to support that either love or affection was Thomas' motive for the adoption. It is interesting to note that, on the marriage license application of Janet Hunt, applied for only two-and-one-half years after her adoption, she listed her natural father in the Father's Name block of the application, not her adoptive father, Thomas.

Each of the parties had an opportunity to submit reply briefs. The various reply briefs added little to the debate.

In the fall of 2004, we began to hear rumors that Attorney Boghossian, counsel for the trustee, had advised Attorney Harpootian, counsel for the adult-adopted daughters, that he should take the strength of our case more seriously, that our brief and the briefs of certain other counsel, posed a significant risk to his clients that the supreme court might not follow *Tinney* under these particular facts.

Attorney Boghossian called together counsel for the various parties on December 20, 2004 to propose a possible settlement of the case. Attorney Harpootian agreed to attend, which, in my mind, substantiated the rumors we had heard. At this conference, Attorney Boghossian stunned Attorney Strachman and me when he stated he thought the adopted daughters only had a fifty-fifty chance of winning the adult-adoption issue—a far cry from where he was when I initially spoke to him in September 2003 about facilitating a settlement discussion.

We were not the only ones surprised. In a December 29, 2004 letter, Attorney Brule, counsel to the Estate of Sarah Hadley, complained to Attorney Boghossian about what appeared to him to be a change in the trustee's position regarding the merits of Hadley Heirs' position. He stated:

> It seems that you have significantly modified your view of this case. . . Renee Evangelista, as guardian ad litem, after the expenditure of many hours and after having been paid significant sums, reached a conclusion which confirms the position taken in your . . . [request to the court for distribution instructions], specifically that the heirs of Art Hadley had no claim. . . . [Y]ou took no issue with the quality of her work, since you failed to object to the report . . . or object to her fee petition. . . . [A]t this juncture, with the introduction of no

new facts, you seem to be recommending a settlement wherein the heirs of Art Hadley receive more than 1.8 million dollars.

Attorney Boghossian proposed that all of the Hadley Heirs (including Ronald Gay and Wylma Cooley) receive 50 percent of the property in the Art Hadley Living Trust, where the only issue to be decided was the adult-adoption issue. He further proposed that all of the Hadley Heirs receive one-third of the property in the Art Hadley Testamentary Trust. This was the trust that had an effective distribution date of May 27, 1941, a provision of existing Rhode Island law that we were not likely to overturn. Applying these percentages to $6,000,000 (the combined value of the two Art Hadley trusts),[13] all of the Hadley heirs would share the sum of $1,000,000 and $1,200,000, or one-half and one-third of the two trusts, respectively. This totaled $2,200,000 to be split among all of Art Hadley's heirs, including Ron and Wylma.

He did the same type of handicapping for the other parties, coming up with what he felt were appropriate percentages. The total of all of these percentages added to 100 percent of the four trusts. Attorneys Harpootian and Strachman and I stayed fairly quiet for the balance of that meeting. Counsel for the Estate of Sarah Hadley and counsel for the Frances Hadley Heirs, however, did most of the talking, arguing why their shares were insufficient and demanding that $400,000 and $100,000 be added to their respective shares. I was struck by the fact, however, that the total difference amounted to only $500,000. I thought to myself that, if necessary to reach a settlement, this difference could probably be covered between the adopted daughters and the Art Hadley Heirs. Nothing was resolved at this meeting. We all agreed to discuss what had transpired that day with our respective clients and to meet again on January 5, 2005 to see if we could settle any outstanding differences.

The fact that Attorney Boghossian's method of handicapping the relative positions of the parties was so readily accepted by virtually everyone, and resulted in what I considered to be relatively few and small differences, evidenced to me that all of the counsel, especially

Attorney Harpootian, viewed our respective prospects essentially the same way.

Attorney Strachman and I were ecstatic with this proposal because Attorney Boghossian's handicapping of the odds of our winning the two major issues involved in the case were more favorable than even our private assessment. As to the Art Hadley Living Trust, we had only to prevail on the adult-adoption issue in order to take the entire value of $2,000,000 of that trust. I went to the conference feeling that we had a fifty-fifty chance of winning that issue.

As to the Art Hadley Testamentary Trust, however, we had a huge obstacle to overcome. We had to first win the adult-adoption issue. Then, we also had to win the date of distribution issue;[14] this required persuading the Rhode Island Supreme Court to overrule itself on a "rule of construction" it had adopted in earlier decisions and had reaffirmed as recently as 1984.[15]

Since it is extremely difficult to persuade a supreme court of any state to overrule itself, I felt we had only a slim chance of winning this second issue. Even if we won on the adult-adoption issue, the Hadley heirs would take none of the testamentary trust unless it won the "date of distribution" issue also. While we had substantial arguments for why it was time for the Rhode Island Supreme Court to modernize its earlier decisions on this point,[16] we did not expect the supreme court to overrule years of precedent. My supreme-court-expert colleague, Lauren Jones, agreed with our assessment.

Therefore, I arrived at the settlement conference feeling we had, at best, a 15 percent chance of winning the "date of distribution" issue. Consequently, we were overjoyed that we had an attorney of Attorney Boghossian's stature arguing on our behalf that we had a one-third chance of winning that issue as well. Since I thought I knew my clients and their expectations, I expected them to readily accept this settlement proposal.

What most amazed me, however, was Attorney Harpootian's apparent acceptance of the proposal on behalf of his clients. Attorneys Read and Bennett, by the end of the session, seemed willing to recommend acceptance of the proposal. Attorney Bigos did accept on behalf of the Estate of Thomas Hadley. Attorney Strachman said he would recommend it to his clients—Ronald Gay and Wylma Cooley, the other Art Hadley heirs-at-law—but he had to first confer with them before he could accept. Attorney Brule and his colleague, Scott Diamond, gave no indication as to their personal reaction to the proposal, stating that they had to first discuss it with their client, Marcia Hanrahan, the Executrix of the Estate of Sarah Hadley. While Paul and Scott spent a couple of hours on the phone with their client, we all noted that they made no counter-proposal beyond the addition of the $400,000 they had discussed at the meeting.

On December 21, 2004, I emailed the Mighty Nine to give them the exciting news that it looked likely that we had settled the case on very favorable terms. I discussed the details of the settlement and other possible demands certain parties might make as a condition to settlement. I was totally unprepared by the volume and tone of the responses.

Everyone was certainly excited at the prospects of settling the case. However, several of my clients missed the point in my December 21 email that they all needed to agree on the terms of the settlement. Five of the nine had various opinions as to what the exact terms of the settlement should be. Two suggested that we make no compromises. It was as if they felt they each could have their own tailored settlement. At first, this appeared to be my worst fear come true: that my clients were going to fracture over the various views of the settlement.

After reading their emails and discussing the variety of reactions with Cindy, I realized the furor was simply the result of a misunderstanding as to exactly what a settlement entails, and that I had left them with the impression that they each had options to choose from.

On December 29, 2004, I wrote the Mighty Nine again—in what turned into a seven-page email—explaining how a settlement works: that I could not advocate one position for one person and another position for another, and that they needed to reach unanimous agreement as to the terms of the settlement they would accept; otherwise, there could be no settlement.

This email settled the waters. Once they understood what they needed to do, they got together and promptly authorized me to settle on the best terms I could negotiate *so long as their collective share of the settlement did not drop below a certain figure.* Taking even the most pessimistic view of where I thought the settlement discussions would end up, we were well above their minimum number. The only question in my mind was whether all of the other parties would agree to settle.

The attorneys representing the various parties met again on January 5, 2005 to discuss further the settlement proposal which resulted in relatively little movement from the respective percentages recommended by Attorney Boghossian at the December 20, 2004 meeting. The Sarah Hadley Estate reiterated its demand that at least an additional $400,000 needed to be added to their share before it would discuss the settlement further. I had been authorized by my clients to compromise up to the full amount of the $400,000 if necessary to conclude the settlement.

I had a private conference with Attorney Harpootian at which we agreed, if necessary, to each add $200,000 to the Sarah Hadley share. While Attorney Harpootian and I were prepared to cover the Sarah Hadley Estate $400,000 demand, we never disclosed this fact because the Estate's counsel would not commit to that amount being sufficient to satisfy their client, Marcia Hanrahan.

As to the request of the Frances Hadley Heirs for an addition to their share, Attorney Harpootian and I did not feel that the strength of their case justified increasing the percentage allocated to them, as recommended by Attorney Boghossian at the December 20, 2004 initial settlement conference. Furthermore, in a previous letter to all of the attorneys involved in the case, Attorney Read strongly hinted that his clients would settle on the basis of Attorney Boghossian's recommendation[17] There was no hint from Attorney Strachman that his clients would not accept the settlement proposal, so we simply assumed that his clients were in accord.

By the time the January 5, 2005 conference ended, I figured we were only $400,000 away from a settlement, an amount Attorney Harpootian and I were prepared to cover, once we received a firm acceptance from the Sarah Hadley Estate and Ron and Wylma. I believed, and I think all other counsel in the room believed, that the Brule and Strachman clients would accept the settlement as well, with no more than $400,000 added to the Sarah Hadley Estate share from the Hapootian/Pfarr client shares. Therefore, it looked like the case was settled without the need for a decision by Justice Rubine. That struck me as fair, reasonable and appropriate under the circumstances.

I scheduled a telephone conference call on January 8, 2005, with all of my clients except one, who appointed one of her sisters as her proxy. My job was to explain the details of the final settlement negotiations, the implications of this settlement proposal upon them and my recommendation that they accept the terms of the settlement. This conference call was pure pleasure because it was the first time I had ever talked to most of my clients. I found all of them extremely bright, inquisitive, courteous, spiritual and fair-minded. I was impressed at how caring and respectful they were of each other.

The call lasted almost three hours. While they quickly and unanimously agreed with my recommendation that they settle, they were filled with questions about logistics of the settlement, issues involved in the case and, of course, what the responses of Ron and Wylma were likely to be.

During the course of the conversation, I was saddened to learn from a couple of Ron's and Wylma's siblings that Ron and Wylma most likely would reject the settlement, expressing the view that the Art Hadley Heirs were absolutely entitled to 100 percent of the value of both trusts, and that they would settle for nothing less. Attorney Strachman confirmed four days later that Ron and Wylma had rejected the settlement proposal. Attorney Brule never informed us as to the Sarah Hadley's Estate's position, so we were all left wondering whether Ron and Wylma alone scuttled the settlement.[18]

At the January 5, 2005 settlement conference, in anticipation of this possible setback, I had already spoken to both Attorneys Harpootian and Read to see if they would be interested in entering into a private settlement with us in the event the settlement failed. I suggested, if the settlement collapsed, that the clients of the three of us, and the clients of anyone else who might be interested, enter into an agreement where they would all agree to pool everything they received at the conclusion of the case, and then divide that pool among themselves according to the same percentages we had agreed to in the settlement. They both expressed great interest in this suggestion as a fall-back strategy.

With the settlement now officially dead, I followed up with Attorney Harpootian to see if he was still interested in recommending this idea to his clients. He was. I felt there was no point in involving Attorney Read at this point until I knew for sure that Attorney Harpootian's clients would agree to this private settlement concept.

My suggestion had one major disadvantage: It did not end the litigation. It would, however, lock in the percentage allocations reached in the settlement for those participating in the private settlement. I spent most of February 7, 2005 drafting a proposed agreement that captured the concept of the private agreement and faxed it to Attorney Harpootian that evening. Since the largest pool would result if Attorney Harpootian's clients won all of the issues before the court, I joked that I would have to switch sides and start arguing for the very position I had done my best previously to defeat.

I had serious mixed emotions about this. While I was, obviously, most interested in achieving for my clients the biggest distribution possible, by now I was also emotionally and intellectually convinced that Rhode Island needed to join the majority of states that blocked an adult-adoptee from receiving an indirect inheritance under their respective intestacy statutes. It was hard for me to accept that I would never have the opportunity to make this argument to the Rhode Island Supreme Court.

On Friday of that same week, Attorney Harpootian called to inform me that his clients had decided to reject my proposal "because it did not end the lawsuit." At that point, I was out of options unless we could get Ron and Wylma to change their position.

I realized how vitally important my decision (not to represent Ron and Wylma) at the outset of this case had now become, and wondered what had lead me to be so prescient in imposing that particular condition when I agreed to take this case on behalf of Ron's and Wylma's siblings and cousins. I have asked myself on numerous occasions whether I could have persuaded Ron and Wylma to accept the proposed settlement if I had also represented them. At one point, I thought I might have been that persuasive. As the case developed, however, it became perfectly obvious that no one could change their minds.

Had they been part of the group I represented, I would have had an irreconcilable conflict of interest between my clients and would have had no choice but to withdraw from the case. That would have broken my heart!

Since I did not represent Ron and Wylma, I simply could not ethically communicate with them in any way. I recommended to my clients that they not put any pressure on Ron or Wylma, letting them come to their own conclusions as to whether to settle. Despite this advice, some of my clients reported that they had approached Ron or Wylma with the intention of persuading them to settle. Allyson, one of Ron and Wylma's sisters, was seriously ill, needed an operation, and had no medical insurance or resources to pay for the operation. She, or some of her sisters on her behalf, appealed to Ron on the basis that she desperately needed the money to pay for the operation, but that failed to motivate him to settle.

My clients reported to me, based upon communications they had had with Ron and Wylma, that it appeared Ron and Wylma's objection to the settlement was based upon their particular understanding of theology. God favored family, they quoted Ron, and said that Ron expressed the view that God would never let the case end with strangers to the family receiving any of the Art Hadley fortune.

Ron and Wylma's sisters soon became convinced that the goal was hopeless—that Ron was willing to risk everything for his principles.

I later noticed the same thing about Wylma: she fully supported Ron and every aspect of his position. Still, some of her sisters told me they believed Wylma would settle if Ron decided to settle; they felt she was in a moral quandary between wanting her share of the Art Hadley fortune and supporting her brother in his principled objection to the settlement.

Having been thwarted at my various attempts to preserve the essential elements of the proposed settlement, I resigned myself to continue the suit through to the Rhode Island Supreme Court and present what I thought might be a winning argument there. All of the other counsel involved seemed to be similarly resigned.

Justice Rubine finally issued his decision on March 9, 2005.

CHAPTER SIX

DARN! OUR CHALLENGE GETS BIGGER

 *John:*

In the American legal system, suits begin and are tried at the "trial court" level, presided over by a trial judge. Under certain circumstances, a party aggrieved by the decision of the trial court can appeal that decision to an appellate court. While some states have more than one appellate level, Rhode Island has only one: the supreme court.

While trial judges often become appellate judges, the job of the two courts, and the skills required of the judges in these courts, are quite different. It is the job of the trial court to go through all of the procedural steps necessary to assure that every litigant gets his or her or its day in court. It is the job of the trial judge to ensure that each party has access to *all* relevant information in the possession of their opponent. The trial judge makes decisions as to what evidence will and will not be allowed. The trial judge also sets the procedural rules that will govern the suit.

The philosophy behind our legal system is that, if *all* of the parties have *all* of the relevant information and have equal rights within the court system, then they are more likely to come to a compromise;

most lawsuits filed are settled before judgment is rendered by the trial judge or a jury.

Before the suit gets to the appellate court, the trial court or a jury has already determined the facts to be used in arriving at a decision, eliminating the need for the appellate court to establish any facts. The appellate court also gets the benefit of the trial judge's reasoning as to how it has arrived at a particular conclusion before tackling the legal issues involved.

The appellate court's job is to determine whether the trial court misapplied existing law or made errors in setting the procedural rules applicable to the suit. The appellate court's workload is measured in hours or a few days, at most. The trial court typically spends weeks or months dealing with a particular case over a multi-year period. The Hadley case had four separate trial judges during the six-year course of the suit.

On another basis, however, the procedural steps at the trial court level are extremely important because any issues not raised at the trial court level cannot be raised at the appellate level; furthermore, most attorneys would rather go to the supreme court defending the decisions of the trial court as opposed to arguing why the supreme court should overrule those decisions. The ingoing presumption is that all of the trial court's decisions are correct. The party losing at the trial court level has the entire burden of convincing the supreme court that the trial judge made one or more errors.

When I first became involved in the Hadley case, the trial judge was Justice Daniel A. Procaccini, a veteran trial court judge. For reasons we never learned, Justice Procaccini recused himself from the case. Justice Rubine, who was a recent appointee to the bench, took over as the trial judge.

Attorney Strachman and I were disappointed with this development. We already knew that we would be asking the trial judge to view *Tinney* in a novel, creative light and not to follow blindly the *Tinney dicta*. We felt a veteran trial judge was more likely to be adventuresome and creative than a new judge on the bench.

All of the parties made it easy on Justice Rubine. We agreed on a single set of facts that Justice Rubine could use in analyzing how existing Rhode Island law applied to this case, eliminating the need for a trial to establish these facts.

The trial court's obligation is to follow existing Rhode Island law, even if the judge personally disagrees with that law; it is not the job of the trial court to establish new law. That is left to the appellate court.

By early March, 2004, Justice Rubine had received the parties' Agreed Statement of Facts and the initial and reply briefs of the parties. Justice Rubine issued his decision a year later, on March 9, 2005.

When I received my copy of Justice Rubine's fifteen-page decision, I impulsively went directly to his conclusion and saw we had lost, at least round one. While I was disappointed, I was not surprised.

Quoting Section 15-7-16 (a) of the Rhode Island General Laws,[19] Justice Rubine agreed with us, concluding that the clear language of this statute barred the adopted daughters of Thomas Hadley from being considered descendants of Art Hadley under his trust documents, since they had been adopted as adults after the death of Art Hadley.

This conclusion, therefore, led to the result that, legally, Art Hadley had no direct descendants after the death of Sarah. Since his testamentary trust was silent as to what was to happen under these circumstances, Rhode Island law dictates that the property goes to his heirs-at-law, determined as of May 27, 1941, his date of death. For this purpose, he was deemed to have died *intestate*.

By contrast, his living trust stated that, in the event he had no grandchildren surviving, then this property would go to his heirs-at-law, determined at the time of Sarah's death on January 3, 2002. This was a totally different group than the heirs determined as of May 27, 1941.

Justice Rubine then concluded that, under Rhode Island's intestacy statute, Janet Hunt and Lucille Foster were Art Hadley's only descendants under his living trust, citing *Tinney* as the controlling authority on this critical issue.

Brushing aside all of our arguments that the holding in *Tinney* does not pertain to an indirect inheritance, Justice Rubine stated:

> The *Tinney* court did not premise its decision on the fact that Ruth Tinney herself adopted Kevin Tinney, but rather upon the court's well established maxim "that adopted children 'are deemed to be heirs of their adoptive parents, as if they were their natural children.'" . . . Nothing in the court's language suggests that *Tinney's* holding is limited to adult adoptees who have been directly adopted by the decedent. Moreover, such a narrow interpretation of *Tinney's* holding would undermine the court's observation that the public interest is served by construing such statutes in favor of the adopted child.

Because the *Tinney* facts involved an inheritance directly from a mother to her adopted son, we believe Justice Rubine committed legal error when he extended the holding in *Tinney* to an indirect inheritance; the Rhode Island Supreme Court had never reviewed a case with these facts, nor had it ever decided this precise issue, so we felt he had no basis for citing *Tinney* in support of this proposition.

Justice Rubine then turned in his decision to the public policy risks of giving a beneficiary under a trust a blank check with which to manufacture heirs by adopting any adult person the beneficiary wants to make a beneficiary. Citing the Kentucky and other states' decisions referred to in our brief, he dismissed our argument and precedents by stating, "In none of the cases cited to the court, however, did the testator or settlor include in the instrument a specific failure provision invoking the laws of intestacy."

This was an interesting statement in light of the facts. In the *Minary*[20] case, for example, which Justice Rubine cites in his decision, the Kentucky Supreme Court specifically found that the trust in question did invoke Kentucky's intestacy laws. The court quoted the *Minary* trust itself: "After the trust terminates, the remaining portion of the Trust Fund shall be distributed to my then living surviving heirs, *according to the laws of descent and distribution then in force in Kentucky . . .*" (emphasis added). This was precisely the same formula Art Hadley's attorney incorporated into Art's living trust.

The interesting point of this aspect of Judge Rubine's decision is that, not only did the maker of the trust invoke the Kentucky intestacy laws, this fact was prominently brought to Judge Rubine's attention in our brief. Judge Rubine apparently overlooked this fact, specifically called to his attention in our brief. This was our second alleged legal error that we would bring to the attention of the Rhode Island Supreme Court in our appeal.

In the portion of our brief discussing Art Hadley's living trust, we argued that the court had the obligation to determine Art Hadley's specific intent when incorporating the Rhode Island intestacy laws, citing numerous Rhode Island and non-Rhode Island Supreme Court decisions establishing this principle. In other words, we argued that the court could not just arbitrarily apply the intestacy laws; it had an obligation, and the authority, to interpret what Art Hadley actually intended in 1940 when he last amended these instructions.

This was a difficult argument to make since there was no evidence available as to Art Hadley's actual intent, except as expressed in the documents. The portion of Art's living trust containing this critical language was probably never even discussed with Art by his attorney. This language is a typical estate planning attorney's boilerplate, or template, used in approximately 90 percent of estate plans in America today.

We had noted for the court, however, that at the time of Art's death in 1941, *Tinney* had not yet been decided, nor would Art have likely considered the adoption of an adult as even possible. In 1941, the presumption was that persons adopted even as minors did not inherit as an heir unless there was a clear intent to the contrary. As a former Rhode Island Supreme Court Chief Justice subsequently involved in this case observed in 2006:

[F]actual circumstances subsequently occurred, *including a significant change in Rhode Island law*, (emphasis added) which Art and Frances Hadley and their counsel did not anticipate and, accordingly, did not leave clear instructions as to what they wanted to happen under the circumstances we now have before us.[21]

While we were quite convinced, admittedly with no evidence, that Art Hadley would have preferred blood relatives to the daughters of Betty Hadley, Thomas' wife, Judge Rubine did not even attempt to divine Art Hadley's actual intention, except to say that it was his clear intent to invoke the Rhode Island intestacy laws in effect in 2002. That begged the question!

After careful and numerous reviews of Judge Rubine's decision, I felt that he had concluded that deciding in favor of the adult-adopted daughters was the correct result, and he then wrote an opinion justifying that result.

Suzanne:

This was a nerve-wracking time for us. How would the trial judge decide?

John advised, "The Judge promised to be prompt if we failed to settle, so I hope he keeps his promise."

Although I was concerned with the outcome of this decision, I worried much more about Cousin Cindy and her failing health. Weakened from cancer and subsequent therapies, Cindy prepared for the worst. She sent me an email on January 9, 2005, "Suz, if I go 'toes up' before trust is finalized, please send this email to John Pfarr."

In it, Cindy named her children as her beneficiaries, along with a note to John:

"Thank you again, John, for your extraordinary endeavors on our behalf. You are an attorney of a different ilk (thank goodness!) and one hell of a guy."

On March 10, 2005, John wrote us an email entitled "Bad, Bad News." John had never sent us an email with such a bleak line in the subject and I was nervous to open it.

"Attached is the Judge's decision. I have not read it carefully yet, but we appear to have lost on both issues and, hence, if it were to end here, you get nothing (Cindy might still take as an heir of Sally.)"

"Oh, no!" I called downstairs to my husband, Don. "We lost!"

I glanced at one part of Judge Rubine's decision, which stated, "Consequently, this court finds that Janet Hunt and Lucille Foster, under the laws of intestacy in effect in 2002, are Art Hadley's heirs-at-law, and therefore Art Hadley's living trust should be divided equally between them."

This felt like a death sentence. The death of a case that John had put Herculean efforts into! I especially cringed at the thought of how this news would affect Cindy.

We'd come so far with John at the helm of our ship. Although the waters had grown rougher, I couldn't imagine the ship would sink so suddenly. We could only hope that John, with his head filled with plans and ideas, could guide us through this storm.

John closed his email saying, "This is not the end of the matter; we will be appealing to the supreme court."

Knowing nothing of the workings of the Rhode Island Supreme Court, I questioned if we would ever see any of Great Uncle Art's trusts. I needed to know more about my cousin Ron and try to figure out his reasons for not wanting to settle this case. I just needed to understand him and what made him tick, before I could attempt to convince him to see things my way.

"Oh, my gosh!" I wrote to Ron on November 23, 2005. "The Hadley case is once more gearing up with advancement to the Rhode Island Supreme Court. Just when we thought we had lost everything to the adopted daughters of Thomas Hadley, it's now my understanding that there just may be yet another chance (gads, how many chances does one get in life!) to settle this case."

In my letter I mentioned the miraculous timing of a settlement for our oldest cousin, Cindy, who had little income and was about to face shoulder surgery in addition to her many existing health challenges.

Not only that, but it was approaching the holiday season. I appealed to Ron's religious side, saying, "Great Uncle Art will beam from Heaven, knowing it wasn't all awarded to the girls but was shared among all of his heirs…and yes, shared even with the girls. I guess that's what this season is all about."

I signed off with, "I wish you and your family a wonderful Thanksgiving and a blessed Christmas. Let's all rejoice at the possibility of good news. Yes, we can all be winners."

Chapter Seven

Where There's a Will, There's a Way

 *John:*

Since we were now destined to appeal
the decision of Justice Rubine to the
Rhode Island Supreme Court, I recommended to my clients that we formally
engage Attorney Lauren Jones to assist
me in the supreme court phase of the
case. Practice before the supreme court
requires knowledge I did not have of a
whole new set of rules. Furthermore, his
extensive experience arguing before the
supreme court was a definite advantage.
Not being a litigator, I had had only one
case in my career go to the supreme court.
I had brought Attorney Jones in on that
supreme court appeal as well. That case
was extremely difficult and had been in
the court system for ten years. Attorney

Lauren E. Jones, Esq., our
Rhode Island Supreme
Court expert

Jones brought us a victory in that case, and I expected him to duplicate that result for my clients.

My clients readily agreed to my recommendation, and Lauren became part of the team. Since Ron Gay and Wylma Cooley had rejected the earlier settlement proposal, it was not possible for me to collaborate further with Attorney Strachman. Involving Lauren Jones was, perhaps, the second of the most significant contributions I made in the Hadley case. In my opinion, his knowledge of supreme court practice and his suggestions on strategy were pivotal to the eventual outcome of the case.

The Rhode Island Supreme Court requires litigants to at least attempt to resolve the dispute through mediation before going through the expensive and time-consuming process of arguing before the supreme court. As part of the supreme court's procedures, the attorneys representing the various parties are required to meet with a mediator and explore with the mediator whether there is any basis for settlement.

The supreme court's clerk's office makes it very convenient for the parties to mediate. It appoints the mediator—usually a retired judge or someone else with demonstrated judicial experience, handles all of the communications with the mediator and the parties, as well as the logistics of the mediation. The mediator does not act in the role of an impartial judge, but instead plays whatever role the mediator thinks appropriate to foster an amicable settlement of the dispute.

Lauren explained to me that the parties in mediation are not only permitted, but encouraged, to have *ex parte* (i.e. private) communications with the mediator without the knowledge of the other parties. The system works, however, only if the mediator keeps these private communications strictly confidential.

This is a practice permitted in mediation that would be absolutely prohibited if the case were before a trial judge. He explained that if the mediator knows all of the relevant facts and private positions of the parties, the mediator is more likely to develop a settlement proposal acceptable to all of the parties. Also, since the mediator is an experienced litigator, he can objectively evaluate the parties' respective strengths and weaknesses. This puts the mediator in an ideal position to predict more accurately the parties' relative chances of winning before the supreme court. Whenever a party is unrealistically sticking to a particular position, the mediator can speak "Dutch uncle" to that party.

While trial court judges can and do put pressure on litigants to settle, it is the job of the mediator to recommend specific proposals to the parties as to how the mediator believes they ought to settle their dispute.

These mediation procedural rules, quite different than those governing a judge, have a demonstrated propensity to produce settlements since the mediator has all of the information any of the parties believes is relevant, whether proven or not, and knows well how the supreme court is likely to view the relative arguments of the litigants. A party to a lawsuit which does not consider carefully the recommendations of a good mediator is generally foolish.

We had the good fortune to draw a great mediator in the Hadley case—the recently retired Chief Justice of the Rhode Island Supreme Court, Chief Justice (Ret.) Joseph R. Weisberger. The supreme court's clerk's office also appointed Associate Supreme Court Justice (Ret.) Donald F. Shea as co-mediator. Soon after the mediation process started, however, Justice Shea announced his retirement as a mediator, so Chief Justice Weisberger served as the sole mediator for most of the critical mediation sessions.

I had no prior contact with Chief Justice Weisberger, although I knew of his fine reputation as a Rhode Island Supreme Court Justice. I came to know him over the course of the Hadley case as an extremely bright, Harvard Law School-educated attorney, and a caring individual who, above all, wanted to see justice prevail. In my years of practicing law, I have yet to meet his equal in ability to grasp many facts and nuanced legal concepts and to integrate them quickly. I presume that this is one of his assets that rank him among Rhode Island's most distinguished Supreme Court Chief Justices.

While the preliminaries to the mediation were going on, but before the process had actually started, one of my clients alerted me and my other clients that the A&E (Arts & Entertainment) cable TV channel would be showing in August 2005 an hour-long program devoted to the Tinney family story. I was curious as to what, if anything, I might learn from this program that would be helpful with the Hadley case. I personally found the A&E program to have little merit; it was sensational journalism showing how the adopted son took advantage of vulnerable Ruth Tinney. What's more, the aspect of the Tinney story featured in the A&E program was not even the same part of the story that gave rise to the supreme court's decision so pivotal to the Hadley case, but was, instead, a companion case dealing with the adopted son's attempts to force a sale of Belcourt Castle.

The program ended with an interview of the trial judge, who decided against the adopted son, calling him an unscrupulous and unprincipled "adventurer" and "fortune seeker," and comparing him to "Uriah Heep," the two-faced, conniving villain in Charles Dickens' novel *David Copperfield*.

Immediately after the program ended, and regretting that I had wasted an hour of my time, I went to my computer to email my clients my disappointment with the program, declaring it utterly useless with regard to our case. As I typed the trial judge's name, however, I had a *Eureka!* moment. Justice Frank J. Williams, the trial judge interviewed in the A&E program, who so castigated the adult-adopted son, was the *same* Frank J. Williams now sitting as the Chief Justice of the Rhode Island Supreme Court!

I immediately contacted Lauren Jones and Attorney Read[22] and told them of my discovery. Both agreed this discovery improved our case against the adopted daughters. Here we had the sitting Chief Justice of the Rhode Island Supreme Court, who was about to hear our case, having previously dealt first hand with an adult-adoptee who he accused of abusing and manipulating the process. We felt maybe we had found a sympathetic judge in the supreme court, who might better understand the risks of permitting adult-adoptees to inherit in an indirect inheritance situation.[23]

This discovery was just one more example of the serendipity that played throughout my involvement in the Hadley case; I often felt like I was being led by someone or something in my conduct of this case. I confess to pondering whether Art Hadley was directing my efforts.

The mediation started on November 17, 2005 with a meeting between the mediator and counsel for all of the parties. At this point, Ron and Wylma were still represented by Attorney Strachman. In preparation for the initial mediation session, Lauren prepared an eight-page letter for the private viewing of the mediator, giving him the facts of the case; our theory of the case; the details of the previous near settlement, including settlement percentages and who caused the settlement to fail; and our strategy for arguing the case before the supreme court.

So far as we knew, none of the other counsel knew they could also communicate with the mediator confidentially; while we will never know for sure, we do not believe any of the other parties took advantage of this opportunity. Our confidential letter demonstrated to the mediator that we had a substantial chance of winning before the supreme court, despite Judge Rubine's adverse decision. It also gave us an opportunity to highlight the flaws in Judge Rubine's reasoning and application of the facts and the unique role now-Chief Justice Williams played in that previous case involving the Tinney family and his attitude towards the tactics of the adult-adopted son.

Our objective was to increase our odds, *in the perception of the mediator*, of eventually winning the adult-adoption issue before the Rhode Island Supreme Court. At this stage in the process, our strategy was to obtain the best settlement recommendation possible from the mediator, believing that his recommendation would eventually be the deciding factor in the case. We knew that the mediator's opinion of the strength of our case would be critical when he fashioned his settlement recommendation.

Most significantly, the mediator now knew how close the parties had once come to settling the case, what percentages of the total each had at one point been willing to accept, and that Ron Gay and Wylma Cooley were probably the only impediments to a settlement. This information gave the mediator a great starting point for developing a settlement recommendation.

While Lauren's letter gave us an initial advantage in the course of the initial and subsequent mediation sessions, the mediator met separately several times with each of the other parties, thus giving each the same opportunity we had to tell the mediator everything that would enhance each party's position in the opinion of the mediator. Therefore, by the time the mediator recommended a proposed settlement, everyone had had an equal opportunity to influence that recommendation.

At a mediation session held on February 17, 2006, the mediator offered to recommend a settlement proposal if all counsel wanted him to do so. We unanimously agreed that we wanted to hear his insight. He then proposed the terms of his settlement recommendation. He essentially followed the same structure that had formed the basis for the settlement proposed in January 2005, except he recommended that the adopted daughters had a 55 percent chance of winning on the adult-adoption issue (as opposed to the previous 50 percent), since they were going to the supreme court defending Judge Rubine's decision on this issue rather than trying to upset it.[24]

While it was a bitter pill for us to accept this reduction in our share, caused at least in part by Ron's and Wylma's refusal to settle, we could hardly quarrel with the mediator's analysis leading him to this recommendation; this settlement proposal, at least, protected most of what we had achieved in the January 2005 settlement conference.

In one of our private sessions with the mediator, Lauren and I made a suggestion that the mediator accepted. While mediation settlement recommendations, and the reasoning behind them, are normally offered orally between the mediator and the parties, Lauren and I suggested that the mediator formalize his recommendation in writing, articulating his rationale for the recommendation, in a format that resembled a judicial opinion. The objective behind this suggestion was an attempt to remove a potential obstacle to Ron and Wylma accepting the mediator's recommendation for settlement.

During the originally proposed settlement in January 2005, two of Ron's and Wylma's sisters quoted Ron as being upset because he did not want "a bunch of lawyers sitting around a table deciding my fate for me." Whether he actually made this statement or not, it made an impression on me at the time. As we approached a new settlement opportunity, I felt Ron might be more agreeable if the settlement reflected the view of an impartial judge, not an arbitrary division of the pie by the lawyers.

To ease the burden on Chief Justice Weisberger, I offered to prepare an initial draft memorandum for his consideration, modification and adoption. I drafted, and Lauren revised, a memorandum of recommendation, incorporating all of the terms of the mediator's recommended settlement. Our joint objective was to show that each of the parties had a substantial chance of winning on at least some of the issues involved in the case. To make sure that each party's position was correctly presented, we gave the other counsel an opportunity to review, and make suggestions to, the language in the memorandum before it was submitted to the mediator.

As modified and finally adopted by the mediator, Chief Justice Weisberger's memorandum eloquently expressed the pathos involved in this case, recognized by everyone except Ron and Wylma. Everyone by then realized that the supreme court could decide this case in any number of ways, that each party involved had a sound argument for why a portion of the Art Hadley fortune should be awarded to that party and that no party had a "lock" on the results. The willingness of everyone except Ron and Wylma to settle this case evidenced that each of the parties viewed it as just too risky to let the courts decide this case. Percentage-wise, Ron and Wylma were relatively minor participants;

the mediator's memorandum articulated the unfairness of letting two relatively minor participants frustrate the will of all of the rest of us.

Chief Justice Weisberger's memorandum began by explaining the lengthy process he went through to educate himself as to the facts and existing Rhode Island law in arriving at his recommendation, including giving each party unlimited opportunity to speak to him and to give him relevant facts and other information. After reviewing the history of good faith negotiations between the parties to reach a settlement, he then went on to give his rationale for his proposed settlement:

> I based . . . [my] recommendation on a variety of factors. They include: (i) the significant loss of additional trust principal that will occur if resolution of this case remains in dispute and substantial additional attorney fees are incurred; (ii) the years that this matter will remain in the court system without a settlement among the parties, delaying the "victors" enjoyment of the remaining trust principal that would ultimately be distributed to them; (iii) the fact that a major issue involved in this case is not entirely settled under existing Rhode Island law and that there is simply no way to predict how our supreme court will resolve that issue; and (iv) the fact that the heirs-at-law of Art Hadley will lose a major portion of trust principal they seek unless our supreme court reverses a policy it established many years ago and has reaffirmed several times since.

He observed that most litigation is the direct result of an action taken or not taken by the parties to the litigation. By contrast in the Hadley case, he noted that none of the parties to this suit had done anything to cause this litigation. While Art and Frances Hadley had extensive estate-planning documentation, he noted:

> [F]actual circumstances subsequently occurred, including a significant change in Rhode Island law, which Art and Frances Hadley and their counsel did not anticipate and, accordingly,

did not leave clear instructions as to what they wanted to happen under the circumstances we now have before us.

I am convinced that there are simply no "good guys" or "bad guys" involved in this case. Art and Frances may have intended to benefit any of the parties here; by the same token, they might have intended to exclude any of the parties here. We simply do not know. My recommendation comes from a heart-felt view that all of the parties to this litigation should receive a portion of "the pie." If this matter is forced to a judicial resolution, many years from now, some of the parties will have won and some will have lost. I personally feel that such a result would be a true injustice, given the particular facts and law we have before us.

He then discussed in great detail the strengths and weaknesses of each party's case, reinforcing his point that no one can predict with any degree of certainty how the Rhode Island Supreme Court will decide these particular issues.

It is important to note that the mediator's recommendation included combining both of Art Hadley's trusts with the trusts of Frances Hadley. This aspect of his recommendation gave my clients, plus Ron and Wylma, an opportunity to share in the Frances Trusts, trusts they had no legal right to share in. Since the Frances Hadley Trusts had $1 million[25] of assets, getting an opportunity to share in those trusts gave the Art Hadley Heirs an extra bonus for settling.

Chief Justice Weisberger then explained why he had departed from the customary practice and memorialized his recommendation in writing.

I have drafted this letter at the request of counsel for each of the parties to this litigation so that they can better understand the reasoning behind my recommendation. . . . I decided to take the time to do this in this particular case because of the unusual nature of the case and in the interest of encouraging each of the parties to agree to what I feel strongly is a fair and equitable way to divide "the pie."

In conclusion, recognizing that Ron Gay and Wylma Cooley were reluctant to settle, he expressed "my sincere hope that all parties to this complex litigation will accept my recommendation."

I was overjoyed that the mediator had agreed to put his recommendation in writing, and for his expression of why a settlement of this case was especially appropriate. Settling this case was strategically beneficial for us. My view from the outset is that all of the parties should share in the Hadley fortune, including Ron and Wylma. Therefore, I totally agreed with Chief Justice Weisberger's view that sharing the Hadley fortune with everyone was especially appropriate considering the unique facts of this case.

As Chief Justice Weisberger so artfully stated, most disputes arise out of the actions and non-actions of the parties themselves to the litigation; here, by contrast, the parties had nothing to do with the facts that led to this litigation. The litigation resulted from a gap in the law, caused by incomplete and conflicting provisions in Art Hadley's estate-planning documents. Any decision favoring one side of the gap or the other would be arbitrary.

Ron Gay and Wylma Cooley were each to receive approximately $91,000 under the proposed settlement. I was mildly optimistic that this much of a "bird-in-the-hand," coupled with the mediator's articulation of the legal risks faced by not accepting the settlement, would be sufficient to persuade Ron and Wylma to settle.

 *Suzanne:*

Sometimes developments in the case occurred months apart. We wouldn't hear from John during those times when he had nothing to report. He's just not a one-sentence-email kind of guy. But when his communication arrived in our inboxes, it was detailed, thorough and thought-provoking.

It was time for Rhode Island Supreme Court involvement. I wondered if the supreme court could demand that all parties in a case settle.

John Pfarr answered my question simply, "No, the supreme court cannot mandate that the parties settle, nor can it reach a decision that just divides up the pie on some basis or another."

He explained, "The supreme court is restricted to resolving, one way or the other, the legal issues placed by the parties before it; in other words, the supreme court will not 'split the baby.' Following a supreme court decision, some get a lot and some get nothing."

John didn't want to risk our getting nothing, and he still remained committed to finding a way to settle our case.

John admitted, "Since I normally do not practice before the supreme court, I am learning the procedure as we go along."

John decided to bring in the best supreme court litigator he knew, Lauren Jones, former President of the Rhode Island Bar Association and highly respected by his peers.

"Lauren will bring a highly experienced, fresh approach to this case, which in my opinion is badly needed," said John.

Lauren Jones' resume shined. He was admitted to the U.S. Supreme Court in 1991, as well as to the Rhode Island and U.S. District Court, to the U.S. Court of Appeals, First Circuit, and to the U.S. Court of Appeals, Ninth Circuit. His area of expertise was appellate litigation, civil litigation and zoning. Lauren received his Juris Doctorate with distinction from Duke University.

Our group welcomed Lauren, knowing any settlement would now be shared with him as well. If he could help in any way, John's decision to add him to our team would be well worth it.

John clarified the role of the supreme court to us in an email in late 2005. "When a matter goes to the supreme court, before hearing the case, I have learned the supreme court actively encourages the parties to settle the case and requires the attorneys to attend a meeting to explore that possibility."

I felt like I sat in the front row of a political science college course or first-year law class. This subject matter never made my priority list of interests in the past, but now I was glued.

A court-appointed mediator, Chief Justice Joseph R. Weisberger, brought hope to the table of lawyers and clients. John said, "I believe you may now be given your last opportunity to settle."

This scared me. It seemed like everything rode on mediation. But John always kept his cool with us, avoiding showing any major emotion. I knew I should continue my correspondence with cousin Ron, to keep our dialogue open and perhaps persuade him to settle with us. Ron wrote me a letter dated November 28, 2005. He knew that our group would be in favor of any future settlement including the girls and respected our opinion.

Still Ron said he would follow his conscience and knew he had made the right choice. He had studied the text of both trusts and Rhode Island law, and just didn't share our approach to this case.

Although I never heard from Wylma, my correspondence continued with Ron as we told each other family stories.

Ron was raised in a non-religious household with his five sisters. However, early on, he read the Bible and developed a strong relationship with God. Ron's actions not only stemmed from his heart, but also from his sharp mind. He was most confident in his abilities to navigate through this case.

Ron ended his letter stating that, after studying all issues, he believed he would win this case.

I appreciated the chance to have an open dialogue with Ron, to get to know him and to hear his views on the case. I also appreciated the fact that, early on in our correspondence, he offered to help Cindy financially.

Prior to mediation with Chief Justice Weisberger in November 2005, John and Lauren mapped out a strategy listing several points in a memo to the mediator. At this point in time, our group was due to receive approximately $400,000 less than we would have under the aborted January 2005 settlement, since the superior court had ruled against us in the meantime, making our position before the supreme court weaker.

John made sure the counsel for the girls was aware of the television program "Chaos in the Castle" and that Chief Justice Williams was the superior court justice who had castigated the adult-adopted son in a companion case to the main *Tinney* case.

The mediator suggested a "fair and equitable division of these trusts." He advised that if all parties involved were to hesitate, there would be a considerable loss of trust principal, and that the matter would remain in court many more years. The mediator wanted all parties to receive a portion of the pie, since it was so difficult to figure out the intent of Art Hadley's trusts, last amended in December 1940, barely five months before his death in 1941.

We were sold—by John's thorough preparation and research and by Lauren's supreme court expertise—which they brought to the mediation table. This was our golden opportunity—an opportunity I felt would satisfy all parties. It made sense. And, it was within reach. We pinned our hopes on this settlement and prayed for the best outcome.

On May 20, 2006, John sent our group an email, saying, "You may have already heard, and I am sure that it will come as a surprise to no one, Ron Gay officially rejected the mediation proposal on Wednesday. Therefore, we have no choice but to go forward with the appeal to the supreme court."

I couldn't believe it. How in the world could Ron reject this! Why would he risk seeing Art's trusts dwindle in value and the case being tied up in court for years to come? A fair settlement mediated through a highly respected retired Chief Justice of the Rhode Island Supreme Court! I just don't understand tossing this reasonable settlement in the trash.

Our point person Cindy, however, had a gut feeling all along the mediation would fall through.

She wrote, "Of course, I am not surprised at Ronnie's rejection of settlement. Knew he would stand his ground."

She thanked John for doing everything possible. "Bless your heart for remaining optimistic. Silver linings are nice."

John concluded, "Now we are off to just plain win the case, or obtain as favorable a judgment as possible."

CHAPTER EIGHT

CINDY TAKES A TURN

*Suzanne:*

Despite Cindy's health ordeal, she maintained her position as point person. She was simply determined to play a major role in the Hadley case. In my mind, I'd hoped this case would keep her thoughts off of her health problems and might hasten recovery. However, this was not to be.

In February 2006, Cindy endured shoulder surgery following the mastectomy. By August 2006, she told her surgeon she felt tingling sensations up and down her arm. He immediately ordered a CT scan to see what was causing the discomfort. The scan showed a large tumor growing at the top of her spine, as well as smaller tumors scattered throughout her body. They tried an aggressive approach with more chemotherapy to shrink the size of the tumor before additional surgery could even be considered.

Cindy didn't always convey her fears to me, but now she sounded scared.

To concentrate all of her time on her health, Cindy knew she had to relinquish her point-person role to our trusted Cousin Wendy. Cindy could no longer function at full speed. The only indication she gave me of her discomfort came in an email that said, "This is a particularly tough day. I'll just stay close to home, hug my beloved pooches and tend to my roses."

Her emails, adorned with little animated smiley faces, appeared less frequently.

Doctors had a difficult time finding the proper chemo dosage for her. In September 2006, Cindy fell ill from the strong medication and spent three weeks in the hospital, weakened and unable to continue with the prescribed chemo. She was ultimately sent home to recuperate and build herself up for further treatments. I couldn't imagine how Cindy could rebuild enough strength to continue with the therapy that had made her so sick, on top of overcoming the cancer spreading in her body.

On October 8, 2006, she complained of not feeling well. She suffered a heart attack and collapsed in her bathroom. Her friend and former husband, Gene Wing, was at her side and immediately phoned emergency. We kept in constant touch with Cindy's daughter, Sarah, about her condition, while saying prayers for her recovery. By October 11, Cindy was no longer with us.

Cindy's memorial service was held, appropriately, in the Little Theater of Walla Walla (Washington), where she had spent years acting on the stage. The service was directed and choreographed by her artistic stepson, Parke Thomas. Cindy's daughter, Sarah, eulogized her mother, describing her life's journey as a series of acts in a well-scripted play. A dancer performed a soulful number, "Remember When It Rained"; a vocalist sang "For Good" from the musical *Wicked*, and Parke sang a fitting and theatrical rendition of "We'll Meet Again."

I felt like I was sitting in the front row of a Broadway production.

In the end, no one wanted to leave the theater. Amidst tears and intermittent laughter, the congregation jumped to their feet, faced

Cindy's photograph on stage, and gave her a round of applause, shouts of *BRAVO!* and a standing ovation.

A second service for Cindy was held in Vermont, where many of the east coast relatives gathered at our grandparents' former home, Glimmerstone. My brother, Robert, played Mozart's "Ave Verum Corpus" on trumpet and Cindy's grandson, Brendan, sang "Wishing You Were Somehow Here Again" from *Phantom of the Opera.* In attendance was our lawyer John Pfarr, whom Cindy had never met in person, although the two of them felt they knew each other after three years of emails and phone contact.

The service gave John the opportunity to meet and get to know some of the family.

"The memorial service for Cindy this past weekend was elegant and moving. After all I heard, I wish I had met her. I understand better why so many of you were devoted to her," he wrote to all of us.

Cynthia Ruth Gay was born March 25, 1934 in Fall River, Massachusetts and died on October 11, 2006 in Walla Walla, Washington.

Our point person, our family's CEO of Smarts and Common Sense and my idol, was no longer here.

I wept.

Cindy Gay

Actress Cindy Gay on
stage; circa 1980

Sarah Dagher (daughter of Cindy Gay) and co-author Suzanne share
a fond moment at the reception following Cindy's memorial service in
Walla Walla, WA; October 2006

CHAPTER NINE

HOW MANY CHANCES DOES
A PERSON GET?

*Suzanne:*

Our mediator, Chief Justice Weisberger, met with Ron Gay to try to persuade him and his sister Wylma to agree to the settlement, but to no avail. Ron and Wylma would not settle, and decided to take their chances before the Rhode Island Supreme Court.

I was frustrated. It was impossible to think that two people could turn their backs on such a reasonable offer to settle. In my mind, it was simply common sense to settle this thing and get it over with. Everyone's bank account would come out ahead. What's not to like about that? Still, I wasn't too worried because I just knew John would have a plan—again!

Since only Ron and Wylma wanted to continue to litigate the case, John suggested a reserve be set aside for Ron and Wylma that they could win or lose, depending on the supreme court's decision, and the balance of the trust funds be distributed in line with the percentages the mediator recommended to those heirs who wanted to settle. This way, Ron and Wylma would have an amount they could argue for on their own behalf, possibly winning it all, while our group would receive a good share without going through an appeal. This was a real break in the case for us; it looked like the perfect opportunity to bust through the constant impasse. John's brilliant suggestion to set aside monies for Ron and Wylma brought hope to us. However, there was yet another speed bump in the road that I never saw coming.

Wylma decided to split from Ron and join our group.

She said, "While I agree with the ethical position of my brother in not settling, I have other considerations that lead me to the conclusion that I should join the settlement."

I was shocked, as I always thought Ron and Wylma were *both* determined to not allow the girls to get their hands on any of Art's inheritance. Although Ron always responded to my letters, Wylma did not. I didn't know Wylma and wanted to get a feel for who she was, so I asked her sister, Wendy, to tell me a bit about her.

"Wylma is deeply religious with a loving family of her own," said Wendy. "Since childhood, she has always been close to, and looked up to, her brother, Ron."

I'm sure leaving Ron's side was a soul-searching and tough decision for Wylma to make.

The case now took a different course, with money set aside for Ron to win or lose, and Wylma's decision to join ranks with our group in the settlement.

John explained to us in an email in January 2007, "Any portion of the set-aside Ron does not convince the Rhode Island Supreme Court that he is legally entitled to, would then also be distributed to all of the other parties."

On January 25, 2007, John emailed us with news we had awaited the past four years. "Two days ago, Chief Justice Weisberger entered an Order settling the case with everyone except Ron. So, technically, the settlement is official."

I felt I was still holding my breath, careful not to let a holler emerge. John agreed that we should curtail our excitement and advised that we not celebrate too soon. Pieces were still moving among many parties involved.

"In my heart I do not believe anything will go wrong, but I dare not let down my guard until this is finished and the settlement is in hand. Therefore, don't let my worry become yours; there probably is nothing to worry about," said John.

John, however, was thinking ahead. He arranged for the securities of the trust to be placed in individual accounts for us that he opened with the Hartford, Connecticut office of Morgan Stanley. The accounts would be supervised by John's trusted investment advisor, Tom Decker, who had advised John and his family members since 1973. Tom's faithful and competent assistant, Janet Ramos, walked us through the mechanics of completing countless forms and was always available to answer our questions and quiet our worries.

Speaking like a loving uncle to cherished nieces and nephews, John offered words of advice. "Within a year after receiving a large sum of money, a huge percentage of recipients have lost most of the money by careless spending and/or fraud. After we have worked so hard to get this inheritance to you, I would hate to see that happen to any of you."

Was our case really coming to an end? This seemed too good to be true, as I reflected on three words of supreme court expert, Lauren Jones: many moving parts. It turned out one part was about to make a strategic move.

Early on, my cousins, brother and I agreed to divide what we received from Great Uncle Art's trust, *per stirpes*. In this situation, *per stirpes* meant equal amounts would be divided among my mother, Alice, and her two brothers, Stearns and Jack, with each receiving one-third. Since Mom had two children, my brother Robert and I would each receive half of Mom's one-third share. Mom's brother Stearns had three children, Cindy, Steve and Nancy, who would split Stearns' one-third portion among them. Mom's brother Jack had six children: Ron, Wylma, Wendy,

Sheila, Diana and Allyson. Jack's one-third portion would theoretically be divided six ways; however, since Ron was not a member of our group, their portion would actually be divided five ways.

Wylma questioned the fairness of the *per stirpes* distribution. She felt the fair way to split our settlement assets would be by the use of *per capita*, dividing the inheritance equally among the cousins.

This upheaval caused another time delay, complicating an already complicated case. This new event didn't feel right, and it worried me. John had to reaffirm with everyone in our group that we still wanted to proceed under the original *per stirpes* agreement. We assured him, we did.

John wrote to Wylma, March 9, 2007, "We have agreed to delay implementation of the settlement in order to give you this second and final opportunity to choose whether you wish to join the rest of us in settling this matter."

John's letter reiterated to Wylma the urgency to either settle or rejoin Ron, and noted the volatility of the stock market.

"It would not surprise me to learn that the value of the assets in the trusts available for distribution is considerably less today than their value two weeks ago," wrote John to Wylma.

Meanwhile, we knew just how frustrated John was becoming from additional stumbling blocks and how his daily diligence to our case was taking a toll. We needed to lift his spirits and reassure him that we were all behind him and his decisions. We needed to thank him for his unwavering work on our behalf.

Cindy's daughter, Sarah, discovered a photo of Great Uncle Art sitting at his desk dressed in a suit. He looked to be about thirty years old and most debonair in the antiqued, sepia picture. Cousin Wendy took it on herself to send the photo around the country so each of us could sign the photo and return it to her. She had it professionally framed.

In March 2007, Wendy carefully boxed the gift for John. The framed photo of Art Hadley, with all of our good wishes, became John's inspiration to complete the case.

"This is the most fascinating case I have had since law school," John told us as he admired the photo each day. John—once again inspired by Art Hadley, a creative genius and a good businessman, and by our confidence in him—kept working diligently for us. His focus, at this time, returned to Wylma.

Wylma now needed to make up her mind quickly and choose either our group and our *per stirpes* agreement, or return to her brother, Ron.

"She decided to join Ron and opted out of the settlement," wrote John, in an email to us dated April 27, 2007.

Although I would have welcomed Wylma to our side, I was happy to hear the case wouldn't be delayed any further and hoped that Wylma, in her heart, had made the right choice for herself.

Now we would wait and wonder about the anticipated distribution.

 *John:*

I was mistaken in my optimism that Ron and Wylma would be induced by Chief Justice Weisberger's memorandum to settle the case. Ron immediately rejected the mediator's recommendation and Wylma gave an ambiguous response. I pondered what to do next.

The real surprise came when their attorney, David Strachman, notified us on January 10, 2007 that he was withdrawing from the case and that Ron and Wylma would be representing themselves (*pro se*) from then on. The rest of us did not care who represented Ron and Wylma, since it appeared that they made their own legal decisions, irrespective of the advice of counsel; however, we were concerned that their lack of legal experience and procedural knowledge would be an impediment to moving forward. On this, we had a pleasant surprise.

We soon learned that Ron and Wylma were bright, courteous, cooperative, personable and eager to learn and follow the procedural rules. They quickly earned the respect of Lauren and me; we believe they earned the respect of the other counsel as well.

During the period they were represented by counsel, legal ethics prohibited us from communicating with them except through their counsel. Representing themselves *per se* removed this ethical impediment. Being able to communicate with them directly turned out to be a positive. From that point on, they traveled to Providence and participated in subsequent mediation sessions personally. They endeavored to be as professional as possible and, frankly, succeeded in this regard better than some lawyers I have met along the way.

In a private conversation Lauren had with Chief Justice Weisberger, Lauren discussed the unfairness of two relatively minor parties frustrating the will of the rest of the group. He told the mediator that I had an idea that would address this. It was a variation of the idea I had pursued in February 2005, after the first settlement attempt failed.

What I had proposed then was that the parties wanting to settle enter into a private agreement to pool whatever they received from the lawsuit and then reallocate that pooled money among themselves on the basis of the settlement percentages. The adopted daughters eventually rejected that proposal because it did not end the litigation.

The idea this time had an advantage over my previous proposal: it provided for an immediate distribution of most of the trusts' funds long before the supreme court would decide the merits of the case.

Specifically, I suggested to the mediator that we figure out the maximum amount Ron and Wylma could win in the case if they prevailed on *every single issue* before the supreme court.

I had calculated this amount as approximately 6 percent of the total of the two Art Hadley Trusts (with a combined value of $6,000,000) for each of them.[26] This resulted in a reserve of $360,000 for each of them if either rejected the settlement. The reserve would be retained in trust, pending the decision of the Rhode Island Supreme Court on the merits of the case. The balance not necessary to create the Ron/Wylma reserve, *plus all* of the Frances Hadley Trusts, would be immediately distributed to the parties agreeing to the settlement, based upon the percentages recommended by the mediator.

If Ron and Wylma prevailed on every single issue involved in the case, then they would take 100 percent of this reserve. If they lost on any issue, however, that portion of the reserve would be released from trust and distributed to the settling parties on the same percentages recommended by the mediator. In other words, Ron and Wylma could still get their day in court without any prejudice, and the other parties could get the bulk of the trusts' assets without waiting for the eventual outcome of the case.

The mediator presented this idea to Ron and Wylma at a subsequent mediation session. While they probably could have successfully prevented the implementation of this idea, they graciously accepted it as fair and reasonable. I recall Ron saying this proposal had the merit of allowing his siblings and cousins to get their settlement without depriving him of the opportunity to persuade the supreme court of the logic of his theory on the case; it was at that moment I concluded Ron was driven by principle, not a desire for control, power or disruption.

At that session, Ron took another step that demonstrated his character. Wylma told us that the matter was causing conflict with her husband; he wanted her to settle. Ron publicly released his sister from any pledge she had made to stick with him to the end. Wylma then announced that she would settle along with the others.

I only wish I could adequately capture the dramatics of that mediation session; twists and turns were occurring so quickly that I felt like a spectator at a tennis match, not as an objective observer. I can only imagine the enormity of the stakes involved for Ron and Wylma as they made their fateful decisions that day.

Attorney Boghossian, counsel for the trustee, Bank of America, stunned some of us by sending out a letter dated February 15, 2007 to Ron, Wylma and legal counsel representing all of the other parties. In this letter, he presented precise figures each party could expect from the distribution, based upon the mediator's recommendation.

Unfortunately, Attorney Boghossian calculated his distribution figures for the Art Hadley Heirs and the Frances Hadley Heirs based upon a *per capita*, rather than a *per stirpes*, distribution, as provided by Rhode Island law[27] and as previously agreed to by my clients.[28]

Attorney Boghossian's letter supported what we were soon to learn—that Ron and Wylma believed that they were entitled to receive, under Rhode Island law, almost double the amount they would receive under what the rest of us considered established Rhode Island law. While he later corrected himself,[29] the bell had already been rung.

According to the *per stirpes* agreement, Ron and Wylma *each* had a 5.1 percent interest of the total amount allocable to the eleven members of the Hadley Heirs class. A *per capita* distribution would result in *each* of Ron and Wylma having a 9.1 percent interest, or almost double what they would be entitled to under a *per stirpes* distribution.

At the next mediation session, the mediator explained to Ron the amount of the proposed reserve and how he arrived at that amount, utilizing a *per stirpes* distribution formula, as provided by long-established Rhode Island law. This is when we learned that Ron, based upon his research, felt a *per capita* distribution formula was the law of Rhode Island, and that he would be asking the Rhode Island Supreme Court for a decision awarding him that.

Since we had assured Ron that his reserve would equal the maximum amount he could recover if he prevailed on every single issue, we had no alternative but to increase his reserve to account for his *per capita* contention, in the event he succeeded in persuading the supreme court to reverse itself and order a *per capita* distribution to him.

At the same mediation session, Wylma informed us that her willingness to settle was predicated on a *per capita* distribution formula, and if she did not get that, she was no longer sure she wanted to settle. We gave Wylma a few weeks to decide what she wanted to do.

In the meantime, as reported to me by one of his sisters, Ron wrote to at least one of his sisters, telling her that their family should insist on a *per capita* distribution formula in their settlement. Since this was becoming such an explosive issue, I decided to go back to my clients a second time and confirm with them that all wanted to utilize a *per stirpes* formula for purposes of the settlement.[30]

They each wrote to me that they understood the difference between the two distribution schemes and reconfirmed their earlier decision that a *per stirpes* distribution was the fair way to handle the distribution.

Finally, by March 9, 2007, not having received a decision from Wylma, and having reconfirmed my instructions from my clients, I sent Wylma a letter, advising her that we were moving forward with the settlement with or without her, and that we would assume she was not settling if we had not heard from her by a specific date. She continued debating the merits of a *per stirpes* versus *per capita* distribution formula under Rhode Island law. Until then, I do not believe she understood that in a settlement, the parties can agree to the terms of the settlement, regardless of the law. This letter made it clear that all of the parties, except her, had agreed to a *per stirpes* formula and they were moving forward on that basis; it was her choice whether she wanted to join them and accept a *per stirpes* distribution or join Ron and present her case to the Rhode Island Supreme Court.

Wylma opted to rejoin her brother and continue to litigate this matter before the Rhode Island Supreme Court.

The settlement went forward without Ron and Wylma. The combined reserve held back for Ron and Wylma, should they prevail on any of the issues before the supreme court, including the *per stirpes* vs. *per capita* issue, was $1,200,000. Suzanne, her brother and seven cousins shared a distribution of $1,600,000.

Art Hadley, age 28; Providence, Rhode Island; 1913

CHAPTER TEN

RON AND WYLMA PUSH ON

 *John:*

With the settlement finally accomplished, I was now in an ironic situation. My clients' share of the over $1 million reserve created for Ron and Wylma was still out there to fight for ($250,000). For my clients to get their entire share of this reserve, Ron and Wylma had to lose on each issue before the Rhode Island Supreme Court. Therefore, I now had to support the very position of the case that I had previously worked so hard to defeat.

My obligation to my clients was clear. In my heart, however, I did not believe Rhode Island's best interests were served if the supreme court ruled in favor of the adopted daughters; this posed too much risk of abuse under the Rhode Island adult-adoption statute. Fortunately, I did not have to deal with this internal conflict. Part of the settlement provided that Attorney Harpootian, counsel for the adopted daughters, would have the exclusive responsibility of representing this issue before the Rhode Island Supreme Court.

Lauren and I were permitted, however, to argue before the supreme court Ron's and Wylma's newly raised issue—the *per stirpes* vs. *per capita* issue. On that issue, I had no internal conflict; Rhode Island law was clear that *per stirpes* was the applicable formula.

Further, I had the unanimous agreement of my nine clients that this is the basis on which they wanted the distribution made. Ron's and Wylma's sisters, especially, never appeared bothered at all by the fact that they each would receive less than their cousins simply because their parents had more children. They did not feel that it was just for Ron and Wylma to avoid the consequences of their parents' family planning. Each of them took full responsibility for their individual decisions to settle, relieving me of an enormous burden should it turn out that pursuing the case to the supreme court would have been more rewarding.

I discussed my internal conflict with my clients. I joked that the settlement gave me my cake and that Ron and Wylma were permitting me to eat it too. I learned my clients had a similar internal conflict, but for different reasons. They were not comfortable with the idea that Ron and Wylma might end up with nothing from the Hadley fortune.

While some were angry with Ron for the two-year delay and almost $400,000 they felt he had cost them by rejecting the first settlement proposal, they were philosophical about the outcome; they felt that, since Ron and Wylma took the risk of receiving nothing, they were also entitled to everything they were awarded by the supreme court, even if it turned out to be more than my clients obtained in the settlement.

This is the philosophical attitude they had displayed throughout the litigation; in one way or another, they each expressed a sense that there was a right and a wrong outcome to this case, and that some higher power would lead us to the right outcome, even if that meant we lost the case entirely. They were simply grateful to have their day in court. This made it so easy and satisfying for me to represent this group of considerate, caring, unassuming individuals.

It was now time for Ron, Wylma and Attorney Harpootian to write and submit their respective briefs to the Rhode Island Supreme Court. Ron called me, asking permission to use portions of the brief Dave Strachman and I had submitted to Judge Rubine. I assured him he could use any of it and that he did not need anyone's permission. First, there was nothing proprietary or copyright-protected about the brief. Second, since it was a joint brief prepared by his counsel and me, I felt it belonged to him as much as it did to my clients.

I envisioned that Ron and Wylma would essentially use that brief, modified here and there to reflect their personal preferences and writing style. That brief gave the Rhode Island Supreme Court the legal basis for limiting its holding in *Tinney* to direct inheritances, thus blocking the adopted daughters from taking as indirect inheritors under the Rhode Island intestacy statute. The briefs actually submitted by Ron and Wylma bore no resemblance to the brief Attorney Strachman and I had specifically designed to appeal to the judicial temperament of the justices of the Rhode Island Supreme Court.

Ron and Wylma each submitted a brief, which was their right. Both briefs I found ponderous, difficult to read, emotional and filled with personal opinions, with obscure legal justifications for the positions they took. As Lauren said in our brief on the *per stirpes* vs. *per capita* issue, "They mixed and matched their ingredients."

It amazed me that they substituted the exhaustively researched legal arguments presented by Attorney Strachman and me for their personal opinions of how the law ought to be, that Uncle Art would have preferred them over the adult-adopted daughters and that the law gave preference to blood relatives.

From all appearances, Ron and Wylma were enthralled by the process of representing themselves before the Rhode Island Supreme Court. They appeared to take great pride in what they were doing; doing it right seemed to be as important to them as winning the case.

They obviously put a tremendous amount of work into writing their briefs and preparing for argument before the Rhode Island Supreme Court. They conducted themselves professionally throughout the process. They learned and complied with the myriad supreme court rules (regarding the length of briefs, the typeface that must be used, how to bind the briefs, how many copies to submit, and so on). When the few mistakes they did make were called to their attention, they immediately and enthusiastically responded with appropriate corrections, and courteous apologies that they intended no disrespect. I had to admire their "grit," and I was not alone in hoping they would win something for their efforts and determination.

For them just to represent themselves before the Rhode Island Supreme Court is a daunting task in and of itself; to do so with so much attention to being as professional as possible, not required of a *pro se* litigant, was admirable. In my opinion, they would both make excellent attorneys, if they chose to do so. In the end, however, I believe they undermined their case by representing themselves. They underscored the wisdom of the old maxim, A Lawyer Who Represents Himself Has a Fool for a Client.

Their briefs, especially, I found were the typical product of the untrained legal mind. They did not demonstrate to me that they knew how to think in legal terms and conceptual legal abstractions. For example, one of the concepts taught in a good law school is to suspend your ideas of what the law should be and apply the law actually on the books. While it is perfectly legitimate (and encouraged) to advocate, even passionately, for a change in the law, an experienced advocate must first recognize, and deal with, the law as it then exists. If a law student cannot learn this discipline, then the student is not likely to be successful in law school or in private law practice. That does not make them right or wrong, good or bad; it just means that they do not think, and analyze issues, the way a good lawyer does.

I remember vividly my first confrontation with this concept in a criminal law class my first week of law school. The professor posed the following hypothetical question. An adult, in violation of local ordinance, rides his bicycle on the sidewalk. A pedestrian jumps out of the way and, in doing so, trips and falls and cuts his finger. As it turns out, the pedestrian is a hemophiliac and bleeds to death before help arrives.

Could it possibly be the law of our land, my mind screamed, that the professor is correct—that this bicyclist could be imprisoned for five to twenty-five years because he had the misfortune of knocking over one of the rare people whose blood does not clot? This result seemed extremely harsh and, at first, did not seem just to me.

The legal principle involved in this hypothetical situation is "we take the victim as we find her or him." If someone commits a negligent or unlawful act, that person is responsible for *all of the consequences of that act*, foreseen or not; if death ensues, then the person has committed negligent homicide or involuntary manslaughter, no matter how bizarre the circumstances.

While the circumstances are relevant in sentencing the defendant, our legal system is based upon the act of the defendant and his or her state of mind. We cannot have a stable, understandable set of laws if the culpability of two defendants committing the same act differs, depending on the health of the victim.

Even today, after more than thirty-five years of legal practice, I find it difficult to hold that bicyclist culpable for such a serious criminal offense. Representing that bicyclist, I would not be doing my job, however, if I based the bicyclist's defense on the unfortunate happenstance of the medical condition of his victim. Instead, I would have to accept the law as it is and show that the prosecution failed to prove one or more of the essential elements of that law; only if I were successful in doing this would the judge or jury have the legal authority to dismiss the case against my client. If the judge and jury are doing their constitutionally-appointed duties, all of the sympathy in the world for the bicyclist's circumstances would not help her to determine guilt or innocence.

What attracted me to the Hadley case was a gut reaction that the law in Rhode Island was wrong, if *Tinney* were extended to include the adult adopted daughters. It made no sense to me that the Rhode Island legislature would specifically and categorically bar the adopted daughters as heirs as a matter of public policy, only to have the supreme court count them as heirs when interpreting another statute of that same legislature.

I saw a potential conflict between the Rhode Island Supreme Court and the Rhode Island legislature. While I went into the case thinking we had the proverbial snowball's chance in hell of prevailing, I was so intrigued by the question that I wanted the opportunity to argue this case and find a pathway that the supreme court could follow to reach the decision we wanted without the need to overrule the *Tinney* case. Furthermore, I thought I saw a way to create that pathway. This is why, while I fought hard to achieve the settlement and used the utmost of my creative ability to accomplish this goal, I was personally disappointed that I would never have the chance myself to argue the merits of the issue before the Rhode Island Supreme Court.

In this sense, Ron and Wylma were my surrogates, and I felt they blew the opportunity to make the legal argument for limiting the holding in *Tinney*. Instead, they chose to make what I felt was essentially an emotional appeal.

The Rhode Island Supreme Court ultimately decided against them on every single issue, meaning that they received none of the reserve containing more than $1 million; according to the terms of the settlement brokered by the mediator, this reserve was distributed to my clients and the other settling parties in the same percentages fixed by Chief Justice Weisberger's settlement recommendation.

Chief Justice Frank J. Williams wrote the opinion for the court. Associate Justices Paul A. Suttel, Francis X. Flaherty and Maureen McKenna Goldberg concurred with the decision. Associate Justice William P. Robinson III did not participate in the case or vote on the decision, so Ron and Wylma lost four to zero.

When the Mighty Nine's share of the reserve was combined with their initial distribution, the total was $1.8 million.

Suzanne:

The order removing Ron and Wylma from the settlement was signed May 21, 2007. My brother, cousins and I signed plenty of paperwork, too, so Bank of America could make distributions to the settling parties.

There were W-9 IRS forms and a Receipt, Release & Refunding agreement for the trustee, releasing the trustee from liability for any reason. John went above and beyond and made it easy for us by opening accounts in our names at Morgan Stanley. All t's were crossed and i's dotted, waiting for money and stocks to be deposited into our new accounts. This day had finally arrived and it was difficult to grasp its enormity.

Now that our children were grown and we no longer had a resident doggie, our house desperately needed new carpets and the faded, old couches in the living and family rooms needed to be upgraded. I also dreamed of a new vehicle to replace our 1985 Chevrolet Beauville van, and maybe a vacation to a warm, sunny climate. It certainly couldn't hurt to dream. Daydreams, though, can end abruptly.

An email from John appeared in my in-box on July 31, 2007. It read, "There is an indefinite delay in completing the distribution."

"Oh, what now?" I thought.

Frustration got to me, as this had happened so many times before; hopes were raised so high, then always crashed to the floor.

John didn't know the entire story of the delay. Like a father figure, he strongly advised, "Don't spend any of the money until you actually receive it!"

It turned out to be a miscommunication among the lawyers concerning the distribution solution for all of the litigants, worked out with Bank of America. It seemed certain miscommunication would occur at some point, with so many lawyers and clients in the mix. At this point, I couldn't help but agree with John; it was like herding cats.

Fortunately, the ship soon righted itself.

"I got word that Bank of America is making progress more quickly than expected, so distribution may be within a week. (I'll believe it when I see it)," wrote John.

He added, "All things come to those who wait, or something wise like that."

My stomach churned at the thought of a large sum heading to our family. It was hard to concentrate as my husband, Don and I, wondered. Would it be cash? All in stocks? Really ancient stocks? How much were we talking about?

On August 23, 2007, I checked my new Morgan Stanley account online that, over the past weeks, had shown a total of $0.00.

This day, we won the lottery.

While our accounts ballooned, Ron and Wylma received nothing. They both sought their own counsel early on, separating themselves from the rest of us, and would forego any settlement. But now, acting as their own attorney, they were still in this to win all of the money set aside for them.

They argued that the girls weren't Art's heirs-at-law, that Art's heirs-at-law under both trusts were determined as of the date of the trusts' termination in 2002 and not at the date of Art's death in 1941, and that they were entitled to a *per capita*, not a *per stirpes* distribution of the trust assets.

John's email to us February 15, 2008 showed a bit of nervousness regarding Ron and Wylma's appeal to the Rhode Island Supreme Court, especially on the issue of the adult-adopted daughters getting nothing. Following the oral argument of the case before the supreme court, John wrote, "I want to prepare you for the real possibility that the supreme court might rule in Ron's and Wylma's favor on the adoption issue."

He continued, "Remember, the supreme court's job is not to achieve equity between the parties and come out with a result that is fair under the particular case. The supreme court has a much greater responsibility than to decide just the case in front of it. Instead, it is establishing law, principle and precedent for all future cases involving a particular issue. Therefore, the justices must have the wisdom of Solomon and make a decision that will properly deal with all cases that arise in the future involving a particular issue."

It would be two additional months of waiting for the Rhode Island Supreme Court's decision.

But then, Wendy's email arrived in our in-boxes on April 7, 2008. With the enthusiasm of a little child finding colorful eggs to fill her Easter basket, she titled her email, "Here it is!!! The Rhode Island Supreme Court ruling!!! Enjoy!!"

I didn't have to read the ruling. Wendy's one-liner said it all.

A cool-headed John wrote, "All of the settling parties (including all of you) share the funds held back in escrow for possible distribution to Ron and Wylma (had they prevailed on any one of the three issues before the supreme court) on the same percentage basis as the original distribution and that Ron and Wylma will receive nothing. What this also means for sure is that it is a good thing we settled."

He continued, "I know a lot of us feel sorry for Ron and Wylma, including me. I know I helped them any way I could. Their actions, however, cost the group of you more than $400,000 from the first settlement I negotiated, and that they subsequently scuttled."

Ron and Wylma had made an emotional argument to the Rhode Island Supreme Court that Art Hadley would have preferred them over the adopted daughters of Thomas. However, as John always reminded us, "The supreme court's job isn't to take sides, it's to establish law."

John admitted, however, "It is incredible what Ron and Wylma accomplished. For two lay people to have learned as much as they did in such a short period of time was impressive to us all. Both of them should consider going to law school."

But Ron and Wylma didn't give up there.

CHAPTER ELEVEN

STILL SOME FIGHT LEFT IN RON AND WYLMA

*Suzanne:*

In June 2008, Ron and Wylma made one last appeal, this time to the United States Supreme Court. Lauren, our legal expert in Supreme Court issues, explained in a letter to Ron and Wylma, "The United States Supreme Court has the power to review the final judgments of state courts *only* in cases involving Federal questions."

John agreed in an email on November 10, 2008, "We fully expect the U.S. Supreme Court to deny their petitions."

It was sad for me to see the walls apparently closing in on Ron and Wylma. The situation for me was more pathetic than anything else. I had truly enjoyed my communications with Ron and wondered how this case would play out for Wylma and him. Of course, to root for them would be to root against us.

I remained nervous, although I knew I should trust the expertise of our lawyers, John and Lauren, as we had done over the course of this case.

Ron and Wylma presented a joint petition to the Honorable David Souter, Associate Justice of the United States Supreme Court, for a stay of the Rhode Island Supreme Court judgment.

Good Grief! Judge Souter's name, a Supreme Court Justice, now retired, mentioned in the same sentence as my family members? It hit me—this is the highest court in the land. I remember walking into the Supreme Court on an unrelated 1995 trip to Washington, D.C. and how humbled I felt, just to see the justices' chairs.

On December 1, 2008, the Supreme Court announced that a panel of Supreme Court Associate Justices had dismissed Ron's and Wylma's petition—their last-ditch effort!

Our attorneys were right in their prediction that Ron's and Wylma's case wasn't appropriate for the U.S. Supreme Court. Ron and Wylma only further lengthened this case, which was concluding its sixth year.

By Christmas 2008, my cousins, brother and I signed another Receipt, Release and Refunding Agreement for the trustee to disburse the remaining monies, as requested by lawyer John.

Just to make sure our group had prevailed over Ron and Wylma, I went to the website www.supremecourtus.gov to make sure that the United States Supreme Court had officially denied Ron's and Wylma's petition for a rehearing of its arguments.

The long and arduous case was over.

I felt deflated. I was happy to receive part of Great Uncle Art's trusts, but I reflected on the hard times that Ron's and Wylma's families must be going through, having many legal and travel expenses over the past six years, and above all having lost their fight. Deep down, I wish they had settled with the rest of us. It saddened me.

 *John:*

Ron and Wylma would receive nothing from either Art Hadley Trust; they had wagered everything and had lost. We could only imagine what Ron and Wylma were feeling at that point, when Ron let us know he had filed a petition to the Rhode Island Supreme Court on April 15, 2008, arguing for an opportunity to reargue his case. As part of his justification that he should be permitted an opportunity to reargue his case, he stated that the Rhode Island Supreme Court's April 7, 2008 Opinion:

…presented no acknowledgment of, nor refutation of, this petitioner's [Ron's] careful study and analysis. The decision also gives no evidence that this Honorable Court actually studied the actual words of these writings [the Art Hadley Living Trust and the Art Hadley Testamentary Trust] to construe what would be Art Hadley's intentions, and to what extent those intensions govern in the present dilemma.[31]

In his eighteen-page petition, Ron did not wait for a supreme court ruling granting him permission to reargue his case; he just started arguing. He began with his analysis of the two Art Hadley Trusts, saying that he had not bothered to make the arguments contained in his petition previously because he thought he had already sufficiently proven his case to the supreme court.

When Attorneys Read and Harpootian submitted objections to Ron's and Wylma's petitions, Ron filed an eleven-page reply, arguing again as to why he and his sister should be entitled to reargue their case. By this point, after Ron had already filed two lengthy documents rearguing his case, the Rhode Island Supreme Court still had not yet even ruled whether he would be given the opportunity to reargue the case. On May 7, 2008, the Rhode Island Supreme Court denied Ron's and Wylma's petitions for permission to reargue their case.

Soon thereafter, Ron and Wylma separately notified us that they each were filing a petition for writ of certiorari to the United States Supreme Court, asking the United States Supreme Court to review and reverse the Rhode Island Supreme Court's April 7, 2008 decision. This was truly a remarkable development.

As Lauren later pointed out to Ron and Wylma in a letter dated June 18, 2008, an appeal of a state supreme court's decision to the United States Supreme Court is not appropriate unless (i) a question under federal law is raised, and even then, (ii) only if the state supreme court based its decision on federal law. Therefore, even in the highly unlikely event Ron and Wylma could find a plausible "federal question" to put before the United States Supreme Court, Lauren wrote ". . . you would still be out of luck."

> For despite the presence of a federal question, the United States Supreme Court will not review a final decision of a state court if the state court based its opinion on state law that is independent of the federal issues and adequate to support the judgment. The Rhode Island Supreme Court rested its opinion on independent and adequate state law grounds, drawn from Rhode Island statutory and case precedent.

> Thus, the bottom line is that you *cannot* satisfy the necessary criteria for securing United States Supreme Court review, which foredooms your latest appellate machinations.

> Given the lack of any federal question and the presence of independent and adequate state-law grounds in this case, we can only conclude that your frivolous "announcements" are presented to harass or harm the now-determined beneficiaries, cause unnecessary delay, or needlessly increase litigation costs. In this regard, [the courts are empowered] to impose sanctions on parties perpetuating frivolous litigation and abusive practices. It is transparent that the purpose behind your legally flawed "announcements" is to persuade the Trustee that there may, possibly, be some reason to delay distribution of funds to the rightful beneficiaries—a delay having no basis in the law, which, given the volatile state of the stock market, may irreparably damage our clients. That is an improper purpose.

The whole purpose of Lauren's letter was to give Ron and Wylma written notification that there were no legal grounds for them to go to the United States Supreme Court, and that, if it were found that they had engaged in frivolous conduct to harass the other parties, prolong the lawsuit and increase the costs of litigation, this could subject them to substantial monetary sanctions. This letter apparently was no deterrent, however; Ron and Wylma continued their pursuit of a sympathetic United States Supreme Court. This they did not find.

Their petitions for writ of certiorari were handled by now-retired Associate Supreme Court Justice David Souter. Pursuant to United States Supreme Court rules, these petitions were assigned to a Conference Committee of Associate Justices for review on November 25, 2008. Without elaboration, the Supreme Court announced the denial of these petitions on December 1, 2008.

In a final effort, Ron filed a joint petition for a stay of judgment to the United States Supreme Court on behalf of himself and his sister to prevent implementation of the Rhode Island Supreme Court's April 7, 2008 decision. I found that this joint petition expressed Ron's personal views more than any of his other writings. Normally a careful writer, Ron shifted back and forth between speaking for himself and speaking on behalf of himself and his sister. The joint petition was signed only by Ron, which meant, as a non-lawyer, he was purporting to provide legal representation to his sister. This petition telegraphed to me that Ron was desperate.

In this petition, Ron put into writing for the first time his underlying philosophy as to why he rejected all settlement attempts. In an eleven-page document insinuating the Rhode Island Supreme Court's motives and competency, Ron stated:

> Why it is that Rhode Island Supreme Court has begun a new tradition of law that removes inheritances from true blood heirs, and then gives those inheritances to non-heirs is a great mystery, especially when the laws as they are actually written show otherwise, and in the petitioners' case there were written actual words that aptly demonstrate and directly instruct as to the intentions of Art Hadley should his first desire fail to be these intentions, thus making his eleven great nieces and nephews, who are his blood-heirs-at-law, the clear and evident desire of his second choice. Unfortunately, nine of the eleven, for various reasons, failed to stand for their rights, but two remain. Are these two to be punished for their careful, respectful, responsible and honoring attempt to claim an

inheritance rightfully theirs, and their desire to see the law properly judged?

Associate Justice Souter quickly denied this petition on December 17, 2008, the same day it was filed with the court. While Ron made some addition procedural moves, for all practical purposes, the lawsuit was finally over, six years—almost to the day—after it started.

Suzanne:

I was thrilled when my brother, cousins and I received a moving letter from our attorney, John Pfarr. A portion read:

> This case has been an extremely important part of my life for the past several years. The most enjoyable part has been the relationship I have developed with you and your family; I intend to stay in touch with all of you and see some of you from time to time.

> We have been through a lot together, which has forged a mighty bond between us. My greatest fear in taking on this case in the beginning was that the group would split apart at some point, and that I would then find myself caught in an impossible conflict, such as would have been the case had I represented Ron and Wylma as well as the rest of you. I truly feel I was guided at the outset not to represent them.

> In any event, all of you have been marvelous. It almost defies human experience to find such a large group with members who stuck together through thick and thin, especially at times when you had some difficult decisions to make. I am not making idle chatter when I say that it is I who needs to thank you.

Perhaps down the road, John and his Mighty Nine can gather to celebrate the Hadley win, look back and smile.

Epilogue

Suzanne:

Great Uncle Art Hadley's original expansion bracelet now sits in my dining room corner cupboard with other cherished antiques. Its delicate links break easily, so the bracelet can no longer be worn. With each dusting of the cupboard and careful cleaning of the bracelet, I take great pride in knowing the family history of the first expansion bracelet ever made.

I also enjoy walking past our local mall's kiosk, the one displaying all of the bright, shiny expansion watchbands, with the sign reading, *Hadley-Roma*. I'm tempted to approach the salesman and say, "My Great Uncle Art Hadley invented the original expansion bracelet ninety-seven years ago. He's the Hadley part of the Hadley-Roma."

I've yet to do that.

Meanwhile my husband, Don, and I have spent the cash portion of our settlement by upgrading our home in Bothell, Washington. We also shared some of the cash with our two daughters, for the purpose of investing. The stocks remain untouched in our account. During the stock market collapse in 2008 and 2009, they lost almost 40 percent of their value. The market appears to be slowly coming back.

Our enterprising cousin, Wendy, purchased a heavy-duty truck and started her own pilot-car business. She now guides big rigs and oversized loads safely along our nation's highways.

Cousin Diana writes, "I never felt a bond, so to speak, with Art Hadley; would he have chosen me to receive his money when he passed? Consequently, I tried to feel what he would use it for, and I kept coming back to education."

Diana will use the money for her two daughters' college educations and has also reinvested the money into dividend-paying stocks, similar to those received from the Hadley trust. Diana is well aware the money came from a settlement and she feels a real responsibility to be a good steward of it.

Like Diana, other cousins are saving their portions for their children's college educations, for investing, or simply setting it aside for the time being.

Cousin Sheila and her husband, Rob, purchased a new home in Alabama where Sheila has created her dream world in the backyard. Rob had been a career air force officer, so this was the first home of their own. As a lover of horses, she used some of Art Hadley's money to develop a child-friendly horse facility, where she teaches "horse-crazy kids" how to ride.

Sheila says, "As weird as this might sound, I love dreaming about what I could do with the money. If I spent it, somehow I feel my dreams would go with it."

My brother, Robert, has lived frugally his entire life. But now, he and his wife, Sandra, cruise around their New Jersey neighborhood in their "new" green 2003 Toyota MR2 Spyder. Great Uncle Art would have approved.

Sadly, our eldest cousin Cindy, who started the ball rolling in 2003, died of cancer October 11, 2006, in Walla Walla, Washington, before the end of this case. She, who could have benefited most from an inheritance, never saw any of the windfall.

Cindy's daughter, Sarah, reflected on her mom and what this gift meant to her. "My mother showed tremendous respect and loyalty for her family. This attribute gave her the grace to present a gift to the Hadley heirs that was not only an inheritance, but a catalyst to create a tighter family bond among distant cousins."

Sarah continued, "I feel a deeper connection to my heritage as I was named after Sarah Hadley, whom I lovingly referred to as Aunt Sally. If it weren't for this case, I may have never found the right opportunity to develop a renewed relationship with Cousin Wendy and learn about the happenings of my other cousins, as well as deepen my relationship with 'Cuz Suz,' who in many instances was a surrogate for my mom. Now my children have the opportunity to develop relationships with their cousins and continue the tradition of building family bonds. This chapter of my mom's life is now closed. I thank Mom for all that she has given me; most importantly, her love and support for both my brother and me, and for passing on the gift of family to us all."

During the case, cousins we had never met united as a team, and got to know each other. We now refer to our lawyer, John S. Pfarr, as "Uncle John."

 *John:*

In March 2007, I arrived home from a business trip to find a fairly large package waiting for me. Struggling through at least two rolls of heavy-duty packaging tape, I finally opened it to find a beautifully framed picture of Art Hadley autographed by all of my clients. Except for a few gifts from my children, I have never been so touched by a gift. The walls of my office are devoid of professional and academic achievements, but I knew immediately I would be making room for this picture of Art. It is an 8 ½" x 11" version of the picture appearing at the end of chapter nine.[32]

At the time I received this gift from my clients, I was a candidate for designation as a Certified Wealth Counselor from The Heritage Institute (THI) of Portland, Oregon. As part of the qualifications for that designation, I experienced what the Institute calls a *guided discovery*, which is answering a series of non-threatening questions over several hours asked by a skilled questioner. The questions are not for the purpose of obtaining information for the questioner but, rather, are designed to facilitate the candidates discovering our core values and how and why we have adopted those particular values (a rewarding process everyone should consider experiencing).

A couple of days after I received the framed picture, Louise Cole of THI arrived at my office to conduct my guided discovery. When she arrived, I showed her Art's picture and told her how excited I was to have received this personalized gift from my clients.

I am a fairly open, introspective person so I had no problem candidly answering Louise's probing questions for a couple of hours, even surprised by several of my answers. Well into the guided discovery, however, I hit a brick wall, and was unable to answer what appeared to be a simple, non-threatening question. This had never happened to me before.

I asked Louise to keep asking the question; I felt something important was about to reveal itself to me. After asking the same question three times with the same result, Louise got up from the conference table, picked up the Art Hadley photograph from my desk, held it up in front of me and asked, "What does this photograph represent to you?"

She had hit pay dirt and, yet, I still had trouble answering her question with anything specific.

Nine months later, still as part of the THI qualification process, I booked myself into a motel 40 miles away for a three-day personal retreat. I brought the written transcript of the guided discovery with me and read the entire transcript three times that Friday. I especially focused on the part where Louise held the Art Hadley picture in front of me, knowing that the answer to her question was the lynchpin for unlocking the true significance of the Hadley case to me. Over that weekend, I made a mighty discovery that has enriched my life since and led me to join Suzanne in writing this book.

Until I entered Harvard as a young man, I was the classic over-achiever. Consistent with how I reacted to all achievements up to that point in my life, I thought to myself surely Harvard has made a mistake. I had held similar beliefs throughout my first eighteen years with regard to my every achievement—promoted over my older peers as a junior Boy Scout leader, selected as the editor-in-chief of my private-school newspaper, which was the first time in the paper's sixty-year history a junior classman was named to this top position. Whatever I chose to get involved in, I engaged as if my life depended on it—not to achieve anything specific, but simply because I was passionately enthusiastic about everything I did. Then life caught up with me.

Beginning in college I found myself more and more seeking achievement as an end in itself, adding notches to my belt, so to speak, as my career unfolded. To any outside observer, my career and life were successful. Internally, however, something fundamental was missing. And finding that missing piece of me has been elusive.

The Hadley case gave me an opportunity, in the twilight of my career, to again experience what I had experienced repeatedly as a child and an idealistic youth—doing something for no other purpose than it was enjoyable, rewarding and especially challenging. It felt so good! I understood; the Hadley case had given me an opportunity to recapture a fundamental aspect of my being that had become buried under a lifetime pursuit of achievement.

What happened to me in my adult life is not at all unique to me; I see it all around me. What I believe is unique is that I got the opportunity to regain that zest for life, doing things at 110 percent for no other reason than sheer enjoyment and challenge, and before it was too late.

When I agreed to represent Cindy, Suzanne, Wendy, Rob, Sheila, Diana, Allyson, Steve and Nancy in July 2003, I realistically thought the case was probably a "loser." It appeared it would be nothing more than a huge distraction from my busy law practice. I was fascinated by the adult-adoption issue, however, and the short-shrift I felt my new clients were getting from the legal system. To me, this was not justice.

In the rush to get Art Hadley's fortune distributed, I felt my new clients were, essentially, ignored and treated by the trustee of the Hadley trusts as just one more step in the legal process it had to check off on its punch list of things to do before it made the distribution to the adult-adopted daughters and the Estate of Sarah Hadley. I was proud, initially, for my role in persuading Attorney Evangelista to give my clients an opportunity to fight for their rights. I am proud, subsequently, of the role I played in winning for them the respect and consideration they deserved. I am most proud of them.

That is all they ever asked for; they were content with the prospect of getting nothing in the end. They were all well aware of Great Uncle Art Hadley, his achievements and the notorious family stories about him. They are proud members of a family of many achievements, of which Art was merely symbolic.

The Mighty Nine was pained and upset over the feeling that they had been cast aside as nobodies and irrelevant following Sally's death in 2002; this drove their resolve to stand up and be noticed. Ron and Wylma failed to understand this in their unsuccessful attempt to persuade their siblings to revolt from the rest of the group over the *per capita* distribution issue. The unity my clients found, and the bond that developed, was far more important to the Mighty Nine than a specific amount of money.

It cost the adult-adopted daughters and the Estate of Sarah Hadley dearly for what appeared to us as a failure to recognize that my clients had a legitimate argument as to why they were entitled to a portion of the Art Hadley fortune. I knew from the beginning what my clients wanted to achieve in this law suit. What they got monetarily was far in excess of what my clients ever wanted, or felt was justified. My personal belief is that they would have ceded far less had they merely sat down with us at the outset and listened to our position and the basis for that position. I went into this case never expecting a dime for my efforts. For me, as with my clients, it was never about the money. We all just wanted to be recognized as legitimate players at the table—win, lose or draw. I was attracted by the huge challenge of attempting to right what appeared to me to be a wrong. I could so understand the legitimate positions of each of the parties to this case that it was difficult for me in the beginning to become a partisan advocate for even my own clients' position. What I learned during the fall of 2003, however, in researching the law and preparing for the presentation of my clients' case, facilitated my conversion over time into that of a passionate advocate for their position.

By the time the research and briefs were done, and all issues were before Justice Rubine (a year and one-quarter into the case), I had invested 250 hours—100 hours more than the next-highest attorney—which Attorney Boghossian, attorney for the trustee, publically pronounced in a letter in 2005 as "unnecessary" for the preparation and presentation of my case—as if he had any idea! I just shook my head and suffered the inferences of his written rebuke.

I was so in the moment with this case, and largely unconcerned for the future or the outcome, that I did not care how much time I felt the cause deserved or what disruption it was causing to my law practice. I was willing to do whatever ethically the case dictated me to do. I have described how I sometimes wondered whether something outside of me was leading me through this case. Was I Art Hadley's ghostwriter—no pun intended?

I was a true Don Quixote, fighting the unbeatable foe, righting the unrightable wrong, without regard to personal consequences. Thank goodness the world is not filled with Don Quixotes, or the world would be in an even bigger mess. For that six-year period, however, it felt good to play that role.

Since I was most interested in simply representing the position of my clients as best I could, and had no particular investment as to the outcome, I never got discouraged by all of the set-backs we suffered—those were endemic to the process. I was simply committed to follow the process to the end. This brought me my joy and my satisfaction for which I am so grateful to my nine clients.

As if this were not enough, my clients bestowed upon me other riches. In connection with my research for this book, I reread all of the emails, other correspondence and documents generated by this case. I could not help but be struck by the fact that almost every correspondence from my clients ended with words of gratitude and encouragement. The icing on the cake came, however, when I opened an envelope from Allyson Gay after the case was over. I pulled out the following: *Ode to John S. Pfarr, Esquire.*

' *Ode to John S. Pfarr, Esquire* '

By Allyson Gay

A well respected attorney while preparing briefs one day,
Was intrigued when then accosted by a peculiar family named Gay.
He engaged his wealth of knowledge, experience, skill and wit;
But held on with uncanny intuition, humor and sheer true grit.

Some strife and varied misgivings unveiled by this perplexing cause,
Served to strengthen his determination and promoted deeper resolve.
His diligence, patience and tactics displayed left me utterly amazed;
So much so, were I in his place, I would surely find myself crazed!

As one by one they shared, he graciously honored each claim,
Soon it was clear they shared only one trait – *no two thought the same...*

Neither settlement nor compromise yielded, regardless of personal cost,
In fact he came back fighting when the 'monkey wrench' was tossed!
Gallant negotiation followed endless research, while firmly refusing to abort;
With genius tenacity he worked it – all the way to the State Supreme Court!

Although I speak for myself - I am sure all the others would agree,
He went far above and beyond the call of his professional duty!
Oh heavens, you ask why so eager, such devotion amongst all the fuss?
Hurray! John Pfarr for keenly representing that infamous ol' Hadley Trust!

The Hadley case was, truly, a tree that just kept bearing fruit. How many attorneys have an ode dedicated to her or him?

I became a lawyer out of respect for and inspiration from my favorite uncle, Bill O'Neal, who was my mother's youngest sibling. I first became aware of Uncle Bill when I was almost four years old. I still have this image of him in his dress uniform as a dashing Marine Corps officer, shortly to participate in the invasion of Okinawa.

After World War II, Uncle Bill went to law school and became a mainstay of the Cincinnati, Ohio, bar and a judge in Covington, Kentucky. He represented for me the epitome of the honored professional who fought with his very being to maintain the highest standards of our chosen profession. When confronted with a dilemma even today, I invoke Uncle Bill by asking, "What would Uncle Bill do in this situation?"

While disheartened by a few in my profession who have prostituted it for selfish gain and self-promotion, I stand proud to be an attorney and of the permission given me by several states to practice in our American legal system. This has enabled me to develop a close, long, professional relationship with a large number of loyal, appreciative clients, many of whom have become great friends. I feel I have been able to make a difference.

The overwhelming majority of attorneys are honest, hardworking and committed individuals who provide yeoman services to their clients. Most clients never become aware of their attorney's sleepless nights, the tremendous stress and personal sacrifices they endure to do the right thing for their clients.

Take my esteemed colleague, Lauren Jones, for example. As hard as I work for my clients, and as committed as I am to them, I do not hold a candle to Lauren. I am constantly awed and inspired by just how much of himself he gives to represent his clients and the causes he makes sure are well heard.

In deciding to write this book, I wanted to use the Hadley story as a vehicle for illustrating just how brilliant our legal system is, and the true commitment of the men and women who make it work. Telling this story has given me the opportunity to illustrate the workings of a few aspects of our legal system.

Despite its numerous flaws, our legal system—and the women and men behind it—is what stands between a civil society and anarchy. Knowing how susceptible I and most others are to peer pressure, I cannot believe the courage the average judge exhibits on a daily basis, continuing day after day to administer our legal system, often misunderstood and maligned by her or his critics.

So, that is the story and why I wrote my portion of it.

Wendy Gay and her new truck; Rifle, Colorado; 2010

Brother Robert Seeley and his Toyota MR2 Spyder; Flemington, New Jersey; 2010

Sheila Franklin's new home in Alabama with barn and field for children's horseback riding

INTRODUCTION

1 We have not used actual trusts' values in this story and have simplified other facts, as explained below, to facilitate the telling of this story. Changing these facts from the actual facts does not change the story or the lessons this story conveys.

We arbitrarily used the following values for the two Art Hadley trusts:

Art Hadley Living Trust	$2,000,000
Art Hadley Testamentary Trust	4,000,000
Total Illustrated Value of Art Hadley Trusts	$6,000,000

In addition to Art's trusts, his wife, Frances, had sophisticated estate planning as well, resulting in a variety of trusts over time. We have treated Frances Hadley as having only two trusts and have arbitrarily used the following values for those trusts:

Frances Hadley Trust for the benefit of Sarah Hadley	$500,000
Frances Hadley Trust for the benefit of Thomas Hadley	500,000
Total Illustrated Value of Frances Hadley Trusts	$1,000,000

The Art Hadley heirs-at-law acknowledged that they had no legal claim to the Frances Hadley trusts discussed in the story. In the ultimate settlement of this case, however, all of these trusts were combined and distributed among the parties who agreed to this settlement, making a combined value of $7 million available for distribution, based upon the values arbitrarily chosen to illustrate this story.

Further, to eliminate complications arising out of fluctuating market values over the course of six years, we have used the arbitrarily selected $7 million value as a constant combined illustrated value for all of these trusts throughout the story.

Complicating the dollar figure presentation further, sometimes the story refers only to the Art Hadley trusts with a combined illustrated value of $6 million and sometimes the story refers to the $7 million combined illustrated value of all of these trusts. A careful reading of the text, for those who want to follow the math, will make clear which value is referred to at different points in the story.

2   See note 1.

CHAPTER TWO: SEEK A SECOND OPINION

3   Rhode Island General Laws §15-7-16(a). This statute states that a lawfully adopted child shall be considered a "child" of the adoptive parent the same as if born to them in lawful wedlock. The statute also has, however, a critically important proviso: "... [T]his sentence shall not apply in the construction of any instrument as to any child who is over the age of eighteen (18) years at the time of his or her adoption and who is adopted after the death of the maker of the instrument." Art Hadley had been dead for over thirty-four years by the time Thomas Hadley adopted these two women. Art Hadley's estate planning documents at issue in this case were "instruments" as that term is used in this statute. Therefore, the language of this proviso clearly barred the two adult-adopted daughters from being "children" of Thomas in the construction of Art Hadley's living trust and Art Hadley's testamentary trust.

4   Art Hadley's living trust stated: "In case of the total failure of ... the trusts ... with respect to the final disposition of the principal of the trust[s] ... , the Trustee shall

transfer . . . the then principal of the trust[s] . . . to and among those persons who would then be entitled to . . . [my] estate . . . under the laws of the State of Rhode Island [as if I] had then died intestate, a domiciled inhabitant of said State. . . ." Significantly, the Art Hadley Testamentary Trust had no similar instructions.

5   *Tinney v. Tinney*, 799 A.2nd 235 (RI 2002)

6   When this case started, the trustee was Fleet National Bank which merged into Bank of America several years later. For simplicity's sake, we have referred to the trustee throughout as Bank of America. In the court filings, however, this case will always be entitled "*Fleet National Bank vs Janet Hunt, Lucille Foster, Marcia Hanrahan, as Executrix of the Estate of Sarah Hadley, and individually, Cynthia Gay, et al, M. P. No: 02-6899.*"

7   Attorney Mark P. Welch, the guardian ad litem for the heirs-at-law of Frances Hadley, made a similar recommendation to the then trial judge, Associate Justice Susan E. McGuirl. Justice McGuirl ordered that the Frances Hadley heirs-at-law be added as defendants as well.

CHAPTER THREE: WE HAVE A LAWYER!

8   Steve Gay and Nancy Miller were mysteriously left out of this case in the beginning. The genealogist hired by Attorney Evangelista to locate all of the Art Hadley heirs-at-law simply failed to identify Steve and Nancy as heirs-at-law of Art Hadley. Once the oversight was discovered, they were added as defendants from that point forward. They suffered no prejudice because of this oversight. For simplicity, we have described the case as if they had been defendants from the very beginning.

CHAPTER FOUR: CINDY, OUR POINT PERSON

9   The same is true for the United States Supreme Court or the supreme court of any state. The holding becomes the law of the entire United States, in the case of a U.S. Supreme Court holding, or the law of the particular state with regard to the holding of the supreme court of that particular state.

10   This is a good example of why we do not generally have "advisory" opinions in
     our legal system. The Rhode Island legislature's position on this issue is a criti-
     cally important factor for the supreme court to know before deciding the Hadley
     case facts. While it might seem fine to extend the *Tinney* holding to an indirect
     inheritance, until a court is actually dealing with that issue, and has had the
     benefit of hearing all of the arguments for and against extending *Tinney* to an
     indirect inheritance, there is a great likelihood that it will reach an ill-considered
     decision that it might later have to reverse because there were consequences the
     court had not considered. As John Pfarr's further research at the Yale University
     Law School library uncovered, the courts of several other states had found an
     abundance of public policy reasons for barring adult-adopted individuals from
     inheriting in an indirect inheritance. These cases were irrelevant to the *Tinney*
     case since *Tinney* involved a direct inheritance. It was only in the context of litiga-
     tion over extending *Tinney* to indirect inheritances that there was an incentive
     to search for and find these cases and then present to the court these important
     and relevant cases.

11   *Bedinger v. Graybill's Executor*, 302 S.W.2nd 594 (KY 1957), See also *Minary v.
     Citizens Fidelity Bank & Trust Company*, 419 S.W.2nd 340 (KY 1967)

CHAPTER FIVE: FINALLY, A RAY OF HOPE

12   The parties seeking a portion of the Art Hadley fortune were: (i) Janet Hunt and
     Lucille Foster, represented by John M. Harpootian, Esq.; (ii) certain heirs-at-
     law of Una Hadley Gay (who was the sister of Art Hadley): Suzanne G. Beyer,
     Sheila Gay Franklin, Allyson Gay, Cynthia Gay, Stephen H. Gay, Wendy Gay,
     Nancy Gay Miller, Robert Seeley and Diana Robertson, represented by John S.
     Pfarr, Esq., later joined by Lauren E. Jones, Esq.; (iii) the other heirs-at-law of
     Una Hadley Gay: Ronald Gay and Wylma Gay Cooley, represented initially by
     David J. Strachman, Esq. and later represented by themselves (pro se); (iv) Marcia
     Hanrahan (Executrix of the Sarah Hadley Estate), represented by Paul A. Brule,
     Esq. and Scott O. Diamond, Esq.; (v) the Estate of Thomas P. Hadley, represented
     by James A. Bigos, Esq.; (vi) certain heirs-at-law of Frances E. Hadley, represented
     by Arthur M. Read, II, Esq.; and (vii) other heirs-at-law of Frances E. Hadley,

represented by Edmund C. Bennett, Esq. Neither counsel for the trustee, Leon C. Boghossian III Esq., nor counsel for the Estate of Thomas P. Hadley, James A. Bigos, Esq., submitted briefs. The trustee had no stake in this dispute and, therefore, was to remain neutral. The interests of the Estate of Thomas P. Hadley were the same as those of Mrs. Hunt and Mrs. Foster, so John M. Harpootian, Esq. was, in practical terms, representing that interest.

13   See note 1.

14   The Art Hadley Living Trust stated that his heirs-at-law would be determined as of January 3, 2002, the date of death of Sarah Hadley who survived her brother, Thomas (who died in 1993). These would include all of the Art Hadley heirs, including Ronald Gay and Wylma Cooley. Therefore, if the Art Hadley heirs prevailed on the adult-adoption issue, they would inherit this entire trust.

The Art Hadley Testamentary Trust, however, had no such language. In previous cases, the Rhode Island Supreme Court had ruled that, if there was no such language evidencing clear intent, the rule of construction in Rhode Island would be to determine the "heirs-at-law" as of the date of death of Art Hadley – May 27, 1941. See *Rhode Island Hospital Trust v. Arnold*, 101 R.I. 12, 219 A.2nd 272 (RI 1966), *Redmond v. Manufacturers Hanover Trust Co.*, 484 A.2nd 906 (RI 1984). The heirs-at-law of Art Hadley at the time of his death were his wife, Frances Hadley, and his two children, Thomas Hadley and Sarah Hadley. Since Frances Hadley was no longer living, the May 27, 1941 determination of her heirs-at-law would include distant relatives of Frances Hadley, but would not include any of the grandchildren of Art's sister, Una Hadley—John Pfarr's nine clients and the two David Strachman clients.

15   *Redmond v. Manufacturers Hanover Trust Co.*, 484 A.2nd 906 (RI 1984)

16   We had only two arguments to make:

First, since Art Hadley last executed both trusts on the same day, virtually everyone agreed that it had to have been a mistake made by the attorney preparing the documents that Art had two different distributions schemes under the two trusts, producing such inconsistent results.

Since Art Hadley had specific language in his living trust covering this issue, he obviously intended the same language to be in his testamentary trust, John Pfarr and Dave Strachman contended. The other side argued just as effectively that *inclusion of this language* in the living trust was the mistake; that Art had intended to be silent on the subject. Since this is the part of the document normally considered boilerplate, the drafting of the two documents by the attorney was probably done without any input from Art on this crucial issue. In John Pfarr's experience, this happens with alarming regularity with estate planning attorneys; it just goes to prove that attorneys need to pay as much attention to their so-called boilerplate as the rest of the document.

Second, in the *Rhode Island Hospital Trust* and *Redmond* cases on this issue, the Rhode Island Supreme Court had emphasized that it was following "the majority of other jurisdictions" when it originally adopted, and later affirmed, in *Redmond*, the "date of death" rule of construction. John Pfarr, therefore, conducted extensive research among the various other states to see if this was still the majority rule and discovered that it was not. For a variety of essentially practical reasons, many of the states had changed their opinions and that the "date-of-distribution" alternative for determining the heirs-at-law was rapidly becoming the modern rule in the United States.

17   Letter dated December 29, 2004. While Attorney Read did not clearly concede this issue, he shared with us a portion of a letter he wrote to his clients recommending that they accept settlement on the basis of Attorney Boghossian's proposed allocation.

18   While Marcia Hanrahan, executrix for the Estate of Sarah Hadley, never committed to the settlement, John Pfarr and most of the other attorneys involved felt that she would settle on the terms proposed or with some minor improvement in her share of the proceeds; Attorney Harpootian and Attorney Pfarr were each prepared to offer her an additional $200,000 from their respective clients' share of the proposed settlement, and they were waiting to learn if that would be sufficient to persuade her to settle when Attorney Strachman informed the other attorneys that his clients—Ron Gay and Wylma Cooley—would not settle on this basis. Fairly or not, most of the attorneys all assumed that Ron and Wylma were the sole cause of the settlement's collapse.

CHAPTER SIX: DARN! OUR CHALLENGE GETS BIGGER

19 See note 3.

20 See note 11.

21 This is a quote from Chief Justice (Ret.) Weisberger's Memorandum of Recommendation discussed later. See chapter 7, pages 63 to 66.

CHAPTER SEVEN: WHERE THERE'S A WILL, THERE'S A WAY

22 While Attorney Read was on the opposing side of the second issue in this case—determining whether the Art Hadley heirs-at-law were to be determined as of 1941 or 2002—we often collaborated on the adult-adoption issue since none of our respective clients would receive anything if we did not first win on this initial issue. Attorney Read is an extremely bright, creative lawyer and proved to be a valuable and fun colleague.

23 See chapter 4, page 32.

24 In his final recommendation as to the terms of settlement, Chief Justice Weisberger suggested that the two adopted daughters share 55 percent of the combined value of the four Hadley trusts—Art's living trust, Art's testamentary trust and the two Frances Hadley Trusts for the benefit of each of her children. The balance of 45 percent he recommended be shared as follows:

21 percent distributed to the heirs-at-law of Frances Hadley

27 percent distributed to the Estate of Sarah Hadley

52 percent distributed to the heirs-at-law of Art Hadley

25 See note 1.

CHAPTER NINE: HOW MANY CHANCES DOES A PERSON GET?

26 See note 1. Also, it is important to note that the Art Hadley heirs, including Ron and Wylma, had no legal right to either of the Frances Hadley trusts, then worth $1 million. Therefore, under no circumstances would they be entitled to any share of that trust, even if they won on all their issues before the supreme court. Under

the mediator's recommendation, however, all four trusts were aggregated. Had Ron and Wylma agreed to settle, their share under the recommended settlement, therefore, would have come from a total pot that was larger by $1 million than the pot they had any potential legal right to.

27   While we will never know for sure what ultimately influenced Ron and Wylma, John Pfarr and Lauren Jones believe that this letter had an impact on at least Wylma's ultimate decision and delayed settlement of the case.

28   Soon after John Pfarr agreed to represent nine of the eleven Hadley Heirs (i.e., all but Ron and Wylma), he discovered a potential conflict of interest between them over the *per stirpes* vs *per capita* distribution formulae. John wrote to all of his clients, explained the difference between the two distribution formulae, and the consequences to them under each formula.

All of John's clients confirmed that they felt the *per stirpes* distribution formula was the fairest one to use. This consent included Ron's and Wylma's siblings, who had the most to lose under a *per stirpes* distribution formula. Therefore, there was no conflict. Had all of John's nine clients not agreed on this point, he would ethically have been forced to withdraw his representation of any of them.

Attorneys Arthur Read and Ed Bennet informed John Pfarr that their clients (the heirs-at-law of Frances Hadley) had also agreed that the *per stirpes* formula was the proper formula to use and the one their respective clients were using.

29   In a letter dated March 9, 2007, Attorney Boghossian acknowledged: "In my opinion, the law is clear that it should be *per stirpes*."

30   See note 28.

CHAPTER ELEVEN: STILL SOME FIGHT LEFT IN RON AND WYLMA

31   Wylma Cooley subsequently also submitted a similar petition.

EPILOGUE

32 John Pfarr's clients later made a similar gift to Lauren Jones. His letter of
March 17, 2009 to John Pfarr expresses his reaction and gratitude. In that
letter Lauren stated:

Over the many years of my practice I have had the great pleasure of receiving
many acknowledgments of appreciation from clients. However, the picture and
notes that I received from the heirs-at-law of Art Hadley that you and I have
been representing is the most unusual and pleasing that I have ever received. It
was a remarkably personal expression from the clients and wonderfully tied to
the case itself.

Glossary of Terms

Agreed statement of facts—an agreement of the parties to a lawsuit or other legal proceeding as to which facts are applicable to the case.

Appellate court—the court that reviews the rulings, conduct and decisions of the trial judge. In Rhode Island, the only appellate court is the state supreme court.

Bench—in a judicial context, the collective body of persons serving in the office of a judge.

Beneficiary—a person designated to receive the income and principal from a trust.

Boilerplate—the portion of a legal document that is considered so standard that it generally remains unchanged from document to document.

Brief—a formal document submitted to a court that sets forth the main contentions of the party submitting the brief, supported by the referenced evidence, laws and prior judicial decisions.

Case of first impression—the first time the highest court in a particular state has the opportunity to decide the consequences flowing out of a given set of facts and legal issues.

Certiorari, petition of—an appeal to the United States Supreme Court to review the decision of an inferior court under circumstances where the U.S. Supreme Court has discretion to hear the appeal or not.

Conflict of interest—a situation in which an attorney has a duty to represent two or more clients whose goals or interests are inconsistent.

Contingent fee—the legal fee that will be paid, but only if and when an identified achievement has been accomplished (e.g. a legal victory, a settlement of the dispute), usually expressed in terms of a percentage of the monetary amount received by the client.

Descent and distribution, law of—a statute adopted by a state that specifies who inherits from a person dying with (i) no distribution instructions contained in a valid will or other proper documentation or (ii) ambiguous, incomplete or conflicting instructions. Also known as "intestacy statute."

Dicta—anything written in a court's opinion that goes beyond its narrow holding. It may give guidance or clues as to future decisions of the court, but is not binding and establishes no law.

Direct inheritance—an inheritance which passes directly from the property holder in accordance with the intestacy statute, if there is no will or trust, or to a beneficiary named in a will or trust.

Engagement letter—a formal contract between an attorney and the attorney's client, required by many states and especially in contingent-fee engagements, it defines the services to be performed and the attorney's compensation for those services.

Estate—all of the rights, obligations and property of a person who has died; the estate ends when the person's affairs have all been put in order in accordance with the law and any estate planning documents the person left.

Estate planning documents—one or more documents (e.g. wills, trusts) meeting prescribed standards and that contain the instructions of a person who has died as to whom, how and when the deceased person's property will be distributed.

Ex parte—defines a communication in a legal proceeding between a party and someone in authority (e.g. a judge, an arbitrator or a mediator) without the participation or knowledge of an adverse party.

Failure of trust—describes a situation where the intent of the maker of a trust is thwarted because the trust fails to identify any beneficiary who can receive the trust's income or principal.

Guardian ad litem—a person appointed by the court in connection with specific litigation to represent the potential interests of people who have not yet been identified, located or even born.

Heirs-at-law—persons determined to be the legal heirs of someone who has died, determined in accordance with the state's intestacy statute or its law of descent and distribution, whichever is applicable.

Holding—the decision of the court on the precise issue presented to, and argued before, the court, and is based upon the facts of that case. Holding becomes state law if the decision is made by the supreme court of the state. See *dicta* to contrast with *holding*.

Indirect inheritance—an inheritance from a deceased person which does not pass directly from the deceased person to a legal heir or named beneficiary, but rather, passes through the legal heir or named beneficiary to someone else chosen by the legal heir or named beneficiary.

Instrument—the Rhode Island legislature has used this term, in the context of this story, when referring to an estate planning document, e.g., a will, a revocable trust, an irrevocable trust.

Intestate—dying without a will or other estate planning documents.

Intestacy statute or law—a statute adopted by a state that specifies who inherits from a person dying with (i) no distribution instructions contained in a valid will or other proper documentation or (ii) ambiguous, incomplete or conflicting instructions. Also known as "law of descent and distribution."

Juris doctor—a law degree.

Living trust—a trust created during the maker's lifetime which can be amended by the maker at any time until his or her death.

Maker of a trust—the person who creates a trust. Also called a settlor, a trustor or a grantor.

Mediation—a process to promote the resolution of a dispute through reconciliation, compromise or settlement.

Mediator—the person responsible for facilitating a dispute resolution in the mediation process.

Overrule—the action of a senior court rejecting, in part or in whole, a decision made by an inferior court.

Partially intestate—the status of a deceased person whose will or other estate planning documents fails to effectively dispose of all of the person's property, due to lack of instructions or ambiguous, incomplete or conflicting instructions.

Per capita—a distribution formula under which all the members of one generation (e.g. the grandchildren) share equally in the property to be distributed. For example, a grandparent has three children: A, B and C. Child A has two children; B has three children; and C has six children, for a total of eleven grandchildren. A, B and C are no longer living. The property from the grandparent is divided into eleven equal shares, and one share is distributed to each grandchild. See *per stirpes* for the primary alternative to this distribution formula.

Per stirpes—a distribution formula under which all the members of one generation (e.g. the grandchildren) share only their parents' share of the property to be distributed. For example, grandparent has three children: A, B and C. Child A has two children; B has three children; and C has six children. A, B and C are no longer living. The property from the grandparent is first divided into thirds, i.e., a one-third share each for children A, B and C. Since they are no longer living, however, each child's one-third share is further divided equally among that child's children (i.e., the grandchildren). Therefore, each of A's two children receives a 16.6 percent interest (33.3 percent divided by 2) in the property; each of B's three children receives an 11.1 percent interest (33.3 percent divided by 3) in the property; and each of C's six children receives a 5.5 percent interest (33.3 percent divided by 6) in the property. See *per capita* for the primary alternative to this distribution formula.

Private settlement—a settlement of a dispute among some, but not all, of the parties to the dispute. A private settlement is not binding on any of the parties to the dispute who do not participate in the private settlement, nor does it end the dispute.

Pro se—representing oneself in a lawsuit.

Probate or *probate court*—this is the court that presides over the settlement of an estate, making sure that bills and taxes are paid and that the testator's property is distributed in accordance with the intestacy statute, if there is no will, or in accordance with the instructions contained in a will.

Proxy—representing another person at a meeting or in casting a vote, with authority to act on behalf of the person represented.

Settlement—an agreement among all of the parties in a dispute to resolve the dispute under whatever terms have been agreed to. A settlement ends the dispute. The terms of the settlement do not necessarily have to follow the law a court would have to follow if deciding the case judicially.

Settlor—the person who creates a trust. Also called a trustmaker, a trustor or a grantor.

Testamentary intent—the intent of a deceased person as to whom, how and when that person wants his or her property distributed after that person's death.

Testamentary trust—comes into existence only after the maker's death, is created by the maker's will and is irrevocable.

Testator—the person who creates a will.

Trial court—this is the court that has original jurisdiction over a case once litigation commences. It is the job of the trial court to establish what evidence will be allowed; to facilitate all of the parties to the case to get access to all of the information to which they are entitled; to oversee the selection of the jury, if a jury trial; to oversee the trial proceedings; to give the jury its instructions, if a jury trial; or to act as the jury, in a non-jury trial, to determine which facts are relevant and accurate.

Trial judge—this is the judge who presides over the trial court proceedings during the conduct of the case. There frequently is more than one trial judge in a case during the history of the entire case.

Trust—a written document containing the trustmaker's instructions for fulfilling the trustmaker's intent. If a situation develops where no trustmaker instructions exist or the instructions are ambiguous, incomplete or conflicting, the trustee of the trust must seek and accept the direction of the court.

Trustor—the person who creates a trust. Also called a settlor, a trustmaker or a grantor.

Trustmaker—the person who creates a trust. Also called a settlor, a trustor or a grantor.

Trustee—the individual or entity that accepts the fiduciary responsibility for faithfully carrying out the trustmaker's instructions as set forth in the trust. The trustee is also responsible for investing and administering the trust's property until it is distributed in accordance with the trust's instructions. The trustee has a duty to administer the trust only in the best interests of the beneficiary or beneficiaries; there is no duty under the law greater than that of a trustee.

Will or *last will and testament*—a written document that expresses the testator's testamentary intent, but does not become effective until after the testator's death and, even then, after the probate court declares it as the testator's "last will and testament." A will may or may not contain instructions for establishing a trust after the testator's death. A will requires oversight of a probate court.

HADLEY TRUSTS LITIGATION TIMELINE

May 25, 1885   Arthur (Art) Hadley is born in South Africa.

December 9, 1940   Art Hadley executes the final amendments to his various estate planning documents, which included a revocable living trust dated January 15, 1936 (the Art Hadley Living Trust) and a will containing a testamentary trust dated January 24, 1933 (the Art Hadley Testamentary Trust) for the benefit of his wife, Frances, and their two children, Thomas and Sarah.

May 27, 1941   Art Hadley dies, leaving his entire estate in the Art Hadley Living Trust and the Art Hadley Testamentary Trust, to be held in trust until the death of the last to die of Frances, Thomas and Sarah.

March 8, 1962   Thomas Hadley marries Betty, a widow with two children (Janet, age 18, and Lucille, age 17), on March 8, 1962.

February 12, 1965 Frances Hadley (Art's wife) sets up her own trusts.

August 25, 1968   Frances Hadley dies.

March 11, 1976   Thomas formally adopts Betty's children as his children after both Janet and Lucille had married and were 32 and 31 years of age, respectively, at the time of the adoption.

September 21, 1993   Thomas Hadley dies, survived by Betty, Janet and Lucille. Thomas had no biological children.

January 3, 2002   Sarah Hadley dies, thereby triggering termination of the Art Hadley Living Trust and the Art Hadley Testamentary Trust and distribution of their respective assets. Sarah had no biological or adopted children.

December 13, 2002   Bank of America, the trustee of both the revocable trust and the testamentary trust,[1] files in the Rhode Island Superior Court a Petition for Construction of Trusts and Order of Distribution to resolve competing claims to the assets in the two trusts (*Fleet National Bank v. Janet Hunt et al* – M. P. No. 2002-6899).

December 13, 2002   The Rhode Island Superior Court (Associate Justice Michael A. Silverstein) appoints Rhode Island Attorney Renee A. R. Evangelista of the Providence, Rhode Island law firm Edwards & Angell., LLP and Attorney Mark P. Welch as guardians ad litem to represent Art Hadley's heirs-at-law and Frances Hadley's heirs-at-law, respectively, as determined by Rhode Island statute.

January 10, 2003   After conducting a genealogical search to determine Art Hadley's heirs-at-law, Evangelista writes to the Art Hadley heirs to introduce herself and to explain her role in the case. In this letter she states, "At this time we believe it is unlikely you will be inheriting under the Hadley Trusts."

February 25, 2003   Evangelista sends a certified letter to the Art Hadley heirs and encloses a draft of her proposed report to the court. Her letter states, "As you will notice [from the report], my analysis of the trusts in question concludes that the heirs-at-law of Arthur Hadley . . . do not appear to inherit according to the terms of the trusts and Rhode Island law."

---

1. Bank of America is the current trustee of both of these trusts and the two trusts created by Frances Hadley, Art's wife. Bank of America formally became the trustee when it acquired Fleet Bank. At various times, different banks have been the trustee of these four trusts. Through acquisitions over the years, Bank of America is the surviving entity; for simplicity, this timeline refers to the trustee as Bank of America even though it may not yet have become the actual trustee.

Early March, 2003   Several of the Art Hadley heirs-at-law, led by Cindy Gay, discuss the letters and report of Evangelista and decide to get a "second opinion." Suzanne Beyer researches online and finds the name of Attorney John S. Pfarr, in Providence, RI, for her recommendation on a second opinion. Cousin Wendy Gay is appointed contact person to engage Pfarr.

March 8, 2003   Wendy Gay engages Pfarr to research the issues and render a recommendation as to what the Art Hadley heirs-at-law should do.

March 19, 2003   Pfarr conducts his research and has three conversations with Evangelista, urging (successfully) that she amend her report to the court, (i) advancing a couple of arguments the Art Hadley heirs-at-law could make under which they would inherit all of the assets of both trusts and (ii) recommending to the court that Bank of America be instructed to amend its petition to add the Art Hadley heirs-at-law as defendants, thereby giving them the opportunity formally to make these arguments for the court's consideration in deciding who should inherit the trusts' assets.

March 19, 2003   Pfarr renders his written opinion to Wendy Gay. In his opinion, Pfarr describes two legal theories of the case that, if successfully argued, would produce a "win" for the Art Hadley heirs-at-law.

March 26, 2003   Evangelista files a Petition for Instructions with the Superior Court, attaching her revised report in which she recommends that the Art Hadley heirs-at-law be added as defendants, thereby giving them their day in court.

June 19, 2003   At a meeting in the court chambers of the then superior court trial judge (Associate Justice Susan E. McGuirl) (with the Art Hadley heirs-at-law still officially represented by Evangelista), the judge, Evangelista and the several attorneys representing the other parties discuss Evangelista's revised report and recommendation. The result is the judge orders the trustee to amend its petition to add the Art Hadley heirs-at-law and formally give them the standing to advance whatever theories they think appropriate.

July 30, 2003   Bank of America files with the court an Amended Verified
                       Petition for Construction of Trust and Order of Distribution,
                       adding the Art Hadley heirs-at-law as defendants, and giving
                       them, for the first time, standing to argue their case.

July 31, 2003   Pfarr agrees to represent nine of the eleven Art Hadley
                       heirs-at-law on a contingent-fee basis, declining, however, to
                       represent Ronald Gay and Wylma Cooley out of a concern
                       that their interests might eventually conflict with those of the
                       other nine. He enters his appearance with the court, i.e., gives
                       official notice to the court that he is the legal representative of
                       these nine individuals.

Mid-September 2003   Pfarr approaches counsel for the adopted daughters of Thomas
                       Hadley and counsel for Bank of America to determine willing-
                       ness to explore settlement possibilities. Both counsel say that
                       current Rhode Island law left no doubt that the Art Hadley
                       heirs-at-law have no legal basis for prevailing in this case and
                       they, therefore, consider it pointless to even discuss a settlement.

September 16, 2003   Pfarr meets Attorney David Strachman, counsel for Ronald
                       Gay and Wylma Cooley, and, after a mutually satisfying con-
                       versation, they agree to collaborate on behalf of all of the Art
                       Hadley heirs-at-law unless and until a conflict arises between
                       the parties.

Sept – Nov 2003   Pfarr conducts extensive initial legal research of Rhode Island
                       law of the issues involved in the case as a prelude to writing a
                       legal brief.

October 27, 2003   The then trial judge assigned to hear this case (Associate Justice
                       Daniel A. Procaccini) recuses himself, leading to the assignment
                       of Associate Justice Allen P. Rubine to oversee the case. As a
                       relatively new judge, Pfarr and Strachman conclude that this
                       was an adverse development for the Art Hadley heirs-at-law
                       since he was less likely than Justice Procaccini to accept a novel
                       theory of the case not clearly within Rhode Island precedents.

Dec 12- Dec 15, 2003   Pfarr drafts initial legal brief on behalf of all of the Art Hadley heirs-at-law (his and Strachman's clients) based upon the initial Rhode Island research. Under the theory of the case developed in that initial brief, the Rhode Island Supreme Court would have to overrule its own decision. Pfarr does not feel this brief is sufficiently compelling to motivate the Supreme Court to overrule itself; therefore, he feels there is little chance the Superior Court would go against existing precedent on the strength of this brief.

December 15, 2003   Pfarr sends a copy of this initial brief to Strachman and to Rhode Island Supreme Court expert Attorney Lauren E. Jones.

December 15, 2003   Pfarr begins working on an outline for a new legal brief during which he experiences an epiphany, leading him to develop a new theory of the Hadley case that does not require the Rhode Island Supreme Court to overrule a critical case decided in 2002.

December 16, 2003   Pfarr and Strachman meet to discuss his initial draft legal brief and its prospects; both counsel agree that this brief will not "win" the case on behalf of their respective clients. Pfarr tells Strachman about the new theory of the case he had developed the day before and a trilogy of Kentucky cases he had found that support this new theory. They decide that Pfarr will research the law of all fifty states to see how the other states have handled the adult-adoption issue.

Dec 17-Dec 22, 2003   Pfarr conducts over thirty hours of additional legal research at the Yale Law School library, including a fifty-state survey to determine how other states have handled the same issues involved in the Hadley case. His research reveals that, under the laws and judicial precedent of three-quarters of the states that have dealt with this issue, the Art Hadley heirs-at-law would win the case.

Dec 23-Dec 25, 2003   Pfarr drafts an entirely new legal brief on behalf of all of the Art Hadley heirs-at-law, arguing an entirely different theory of the case that came out of the additional research. Under the new theory, it would not be necessary for the Rhode Island Supreme Courts to overrule existing precedent.

December 26, 2003   Pfarr begins drafting an annotation of his fifty-state survey that shows the overwhelming majority of states would have resolved this case in favor of the Pfarr/Strachman clients.

Jan 12-Jan 30, 2004   Pfarr and Strachman meet frequently to edit and refine the legal brief and the annotation recording the results of Pfarr's fifty-state survey.

Early February 2004   Briefs of all parties are filed with the Superior Court. Pfarr and Strachman submit their collaborative effort, attaching Pfarr's annotation of his fifty-state survey in support of their joint brief.

December 20, 2004 & January 5, 2005   All counsel involved in the case have two day-long conferences to discuss a settlement of the case; all but three parties agree to a settlement of the case, based upon the legal briefs submitted. Under the proposed settlement, the Art Hadley heirs-at-law would divide $2 million, which represents two-fifths of the then-combined value of the Art Hadley Living Trust and the Art Hadley Testamentary Trust. Ron Gay and Wylma Cooley reject the proposed settlement outright. The Estate of Sarah Hadley neither accepts nor rejects the settlement in light of the position of Gay and Cooley. The combined interest of Gay and Cooley in the case represents a relatively small percentage of the total, yet a settlement requires 100 percent agreement. This position of Gay/Cooley creates the conflict of interest that has long concerned Pfarr, resulting in the termination of the collaboration between Pfarr and Strachman.

January 12, 2005   Strachman sends a letter to all counsel formally rejecting the settlement proposal on behalf of Gay and Cooley.

Jan 5-Feb 11, 2005   Pfarr proposes and then pursues the concept of a "private" settlement to the counsel for the two adopted daughters, Attorney John Harpootian, and counsel for eight of the Frances Hadley Heirs, Attorney Arthur Read. Under his proposal, their respective clients would combine whatever share of the trusts were eventually awarded to them by the court and then share those awards on the same basis as they had agreed to under the aborted settlement proposal. After it initially looks like the two adopted daughters will agree—to the point of Pfarr drafting the necessary documentation—the daughters ultimately back out of the agreement because it would not avoid the need to continue the litigation to the Rhode Island Supreme Court.

March 9, 2005   Justice Rubine issues his decision in the case. While he agrees that, under Rhode Island statutory law, the Art Hadley heirs-at-law would defeat the position of the adopted daughters, he rules that a Rhode Island Supreme Court decision rendered in 2002 supplants the statutory rule and, therefore, he awards to the adopted daughters all of the proceeds of Thomas Hadley's share of the trusts' assets. While the Art Hadley heirs-at-law are disappointed by Rubine's decision, Pfarr informs them that he will be appealing Rubine's decision to the Rhode Island Supreme Court.

April 26, 2005   On the recommendation of Pfarr, his clients authorize him to engage Rhode Island Supreme Court expert—Attorney Lauren E. Jones, to work with him to represent their interests before the Rhode Island Supreme Court.

July 2005   Since none of the parties with a financial stake in the outcome of this case are completely satisfied with Rubine's decision, all counsel file an appeal of Rubine's decision to the Rhode Island Supreme Court.

August 19, 2005   A&E (Arts & Entertainment) airs a television program about the same facts that gave rise to the 2002 Rhode Island Supreme Court decision that was causing such an obstacle to the Art Hadley heirs-at-law. Pfarr learns by watching this program that the superior court judge hearing that case before it went to the Supreme Court—Judge Frank J. Williams—appears to agree with the Art Hadley heirs-at-law on the potential abuse that can come from letting adult-adoptees inherit. The significance of this discovery is that, by the time the Hadley case is about to be heard by the Rhode Island Supreme Court—Judge Frank J. Williams—is the Chief Justice of the Rhode Island Supreme Court.

October 3, 2005   Under Rhode Island Supreme Court rules, the supreme court submits the dispute to mediation before a retired Chief Justice of the Rhode Island Supreme Court, Chief Justice (Ret.) Joseph

R. Weisberger, and a retired Rhode Island Associate Supreme Court Judge, Justice Donald F. Shea.

November 17, 2005   First mediation session with mediators Weisberger and Shea. Shea announces that he will shortly be retiring from the supreme court's mediation program. Weisberger handles the Hadley case mediation alone after this initial session.

January 4, 2006   Weisberger conducts mediation session, holding a private conversation with each of the parties having a financial stake in the litigation.

February 17, 2006   Counsel for all parties meet with Weisberger to discuss a settlement of the case in lieu of having the supreme court decide the case. Under the recommendation of Weisberger, the Art Hadley heirs-at-law would receive $400,000 less than they would have received under the aborted January 2005 settlement proposal; this reduction reflects the fact that, in the interim, Justice Rubine had ruled against them, making their position before the supreme court weaker., Pfarr makes counsel for the two adopted daughters aware of the A&E program aired on August 19, 2005 and that now-Chief Justice Williams was the superior court justice in that case. All of the parties, with the exception of Gay and Cooley, agree to Weisberger's recommended settlement. Pfarr and Jones privately recommend to Weisberger that he put his recommendation in writing so that Gay and Cooley will see that his settlement recommendation is "fair and equitable" in the opinion of an experienced litigator and former supreme court chief justice rather than an arbitrary division of the "pie" by the attorneys in the case.

April 4, 2006   Weisberger issues a written recommendation as to the reasons why he urges all parties to settle the case on the basis he had proposed. This recommendation is initially drafted by Pfarr, edited by Jones, and adopted with changes by Weisberger. Strachman informs Weisberger that his clients probably will reject his proposed settlement. Weisberger asks Strachman if he can arrange a meeting between him and Gay and Cooley.

April 11, 2006   Weisberger meets with Gay in an attempt to persuade Gay and Cooley to agree to the settlement.

May 17, 2006   At a mediation session, Strachman notifies Weisberger and the other counsel that Gay and Cooley reject the settlement and that they will be taking their chances before the supreme court.

May 2006   Jones expresses to Weisberger great frustration that the relatively minor interest of Gay and Cooley can frustrate the will and desire of the other parties to settle the case. Jones tells Weisberger that Pfarr has an idea of how Gay/Cooley can continue their appeal to the supreme court and the other parties can take currently the majority of the distribution contemplated by Weisberger's settlement proposal.

May 2006   Pfarr describes to Weisberger his suggestion that (i) the highest amount of assets, representing the "best case" result for Gay and Cooley, be placed in escrow until the final resolution of the case by the supreme court and (ii) the balance of the assets in these trusts be distributed to the parties who have agreed to settle. This is a variation of the idea Pfarr attempted to implement in January-February 2005 after the initial settlement proposal was rejected by Gay and Cooley.

January 10, 2007   Strachman withdraws as counsel for Gay and Cooley. Gay and Cooley file documentation with the court that they will represent themselves (pro se) in the future.

January 19, 2007   A meeting of all parties is held by Weisberger to discuss the proposal put forth by Pfarr permitting a settlement among all of the parties who want to settle and, yet, preserving Gay's and Cooley's right to pursue their appeal to the Rhode Island Supreme Court. The proposal is adopted by Gay, reaffirming that he will not be a party to this distribution. Cooley announces that she will accept the settlement.

January 24, 2007   Weisberger issues an order to distribute the assets in the four Hadley trusts except for a reserve created to protect Gay in the event he prevails on any of three issues he will be appealing to the supreme court. Gay is permitted under this order to pursue his appeal. The order establishes deadlines for filing supreme court briefs by Harpootian, Gay and the other parties.

January-April 2007	Cooley announces that her decision to settle was predicated on the assumption that the distribution would be *per capita*. If the distribution is to be *per stirpes*, as agreed to by all of the other parties, she expressed uncertainty as to whether she was willing to settle.
March 9, 2007	Pfarr sends a letter to Cooley advising her that the time has come for her to decide finally whether (i) she wants to settle on the same *per stirpes* basis as the other parties or (ii) rejoin Gay and pursue her appeal to the supreme court.
April 27, 2007	At mediation session, Cooley announces that she has decided not to settle and to join Gay in pursuing an appeal to the supreme court.
May 21, 2007	Weisberger issues a supplement to his January 24, 2007 order removing Cooley from the settlement, permitting her to pursue her appeal to the supreme court.
June 6, 2007	Weisberger issues a distribution order directing distribution of all of the trusts' assets to the settling parties pursuant to the settlement, with the exception of a reserve held back to protect Gay and Cooley in the event they win on any of the three issues they will be presenting to the supreme court.
Mar–Dec 2007	Gay, Cooley, Harpootian and Jones submit their legal briefs to the Rhode Island Supreme Court. The Jones brief is restricted to the *per stirpes* vs. *per capita* issue; supreme court rules do not permit a party to take a position that is inconsistent with the position taken before the trial court.
August 28, 2007	Bank of America begins distribution of all of the trusts' assets to all of the settling parties, holding back only the reserve created to protect Gay and Cooley and for final administrative expenses of the trustee.
March 10, 2008	Oral argument is held before the Rhode Island Supreme Court. Harpootian argues on behalf of the adopted daughters. Jones argues on behalf of the settling-parties on the *per stirpes* vs

per capita distribution issue. Gay and Cooley argue on their own behalf.

April 7, 2008	Rhode Island Supreme Court issues its decision, ruling that Gay and Cooley take nothing from the Art Hadley Living Trust or the Art Hadley Testamentary Trust. Under the settlement agreed to by all of the other parties, the reserve held for the benefit of Gay and Cooley, in the event they won on any of the issues they appealed to the supreme court, is to be distributed to all of the settling parties pursuant to the same percentages agreed to in the settlement as recommended by Weisberger. Gay and Cooley receive nothing, whereas they had rejected many attempts to settle, including the opportunity to receive their shares of the $2 million proposed in the January 2005 aborted settlement proposal. The supreme court did not rule on the Gay/Cooley contention that the distribution should be *per capita* rather than *per stirpes*; since there is nothing to distribute to Gay/Cooley, that issue is moot.
April 15, 2008	Gay files petition with the supreme court for permission to reargue his case; without waiting for the permission to reargue his case that he sought, he used this petition to reargue his case.
April 2008	Cooley files petition with the supreme court for permission to reargue her case.
April 2008	Harpootian and Read file objections to Gay's and Cooley's petitions for permission to reargue their case; Gay and Cooley, without waiting for permission to reargue their case, Gay begins again to make his reargument on behalf of Cooley and himself.
May 7, 2008	Rhode Island Supreme Court issues order denying Gay's/Cooley's request for permission to reargue their case.
May 2008	Gay and Cooley announce intent to appeal case to the United States Supreme Court. In response, supreme court expert Jones sends a letter to Gay/Cooley explaining why the United States Supreme Court has no jurisdiction to hear this case and that they face severe financial sanctions if their United States Supreme Court appeal is found to be for frivolous purposes.

December 1, 2008	United States Supreme Court rejects various attempts by Gay/Cooley to persuade the United States Supreme Court to hear their appeal.
December 17, 2008	Gay and Cooley file a petition with the United States Supreme Court to reconsider its decision not to hear the Gay/Cooley appeal.
December 17, 2008	Associate Justice David Souter denies the Gay/Cooley petition that the supreme court reconsider its decision.
Jan–Sept 2009	The trustee resolves a variety of administration issues as a prelude to making a final distribution of the four Hadley trusts.
September 15, 2009	The settling parties begin receiving from Bank of America the Gay/Cooley reserve they became entitled to once the Rhode Island Supreme Court ruled against Gay and Cooley.

Hadley Jewelry Company Timeline

1905	The Hadley Jewelry Company is established at 26 Fountain Street, Providence, Rhode Island.
February 11, 1913	Art Hadley's expansion bracelet invention is patented.
1937	Art Hadley retires from Hadley Jewelry Company and his optical company in England.
May 27, 1941	Art Hadley dies at the age of fifty-six. George Ingleby becomes president of the Hadley Jewelry Company.
1950 – 1960	Elgin National Watch Company purchases and owns the Hadley Jewelry Company.
1960	Bertram Kalisher acquires the Hadley Watchband Company (originally Hadley Jewelry Company) that was owned by Elgin National Watch Company. Kalisher retains the Hadley name and calls the company Hadley Kalbé.
1986	Roma Industries purchases Hadley Kalbé. The company today is called Hadley-Roma, with the founder's name, Hadley, firmly in place. Hadley-Roma is the largest watchband company in the United States.

ACKNOWLEDGEMENTS

B ehind every story, a team effort and a wide range of talent mold the tale into a cohesive final result.

Suzanne:

I thank and appreciate so much, my husband, Don, for his unwavering support throughout this case and his positive encouragement at all times on this book project. I couldn't have tackled writing the book without his technical expertise in everything "computer" and the many hours he spent retouching and scanning the old family photos.

I thank my brother Robert Seeley and cousins Wendy Gay, Sheila Franklin, Diana Robertson, Allyson Gay, Nancy Miller, Steve Gay, Cindy Gay and Cindy's daughter, Sarah Dagher, for unifying as a cohesive, family team during this six-year legal case, which made it possible for us all to share in a portion of our great uncle's legacy.

Bertram Kalisher, thank you for your generosity and enthusiasm in sharing information about Art Hadley's genius, the importance of the expansion bracelet invention and for your knowledge of the Hadley Jewelry Company!

I give a loud shout of *BRAVO!* to Attorney Lauren E. Jones, Esq., who guided John and our group through complex Rhode Island Supreme Court procedures.

 *John:*

As we were developing the final brief we submitted to the court in the early stages of this case, three of my favorite attorneys served me as invaluable devil's advocates as I bounced ideas and alternative theories off of them and received their insightful reactions. They are: Arthur "Art" L. Stern, III, Esq., of Tallahassee, Florida; Bernard "Bernie" M. Rethore, Esq., of Paradise Valley, Arizona; and Lauren E. Jones, Esq., of Providence, Rhode Island. Thank you, Art, Bernie and Lauren.

At a critical point after the settlement concluded, and when we encountered logistical problems with the distribution itself from the trustee, I turned to trusted advisors and friends at Morgan Stanley Smith Barney—Tom Decker and Janet Ramos—who opened, on an expedited basis, accounts for each of my clients in order to funnel the distributed funds to a single institution for redistribution to their individual accounts. Janet, first recognizing that Bank of America was using the wrong procedures and forms, used her knowledge of the industry to get the problem rectified and the distribution back on track. Tom and Janet, I thank you for rushing in to help me out of a difficult spot and for little or no personal compensation.

The terms of the settlement in the Hadley case were easy to express in words; it was an entirely different matter, however, reducing it all to dollar amounts. This required spreadsheets with complicated (for me) formulae properly reallocating first Ronald Gay's reserve among certain of the other parties, and then making a similar reallocation of Wylma Cooley's reserve. I lacked the mathematical skill to develop all of these formulae and turned to my colleague, Mary C. Foretich, C.P.A., of Mesa, Arizona, who took the time to understand the case and all of the settlement terms. She then helped me resolve how to the handle the Ron/Wylma situation and finally developed the formulae needed to reflect the settlement terms properly on a spreadsheet. Without Mary, I would have had to find someone else to help me or go back to pre-spreadsheet technology to figure this all out. Thank you, Mary.

My assistant, Janis M. Tangney, of East Lyme, Connecticut, was at my side during this saga from early 2007 through the conclusion of the case, the clean-up of the aftermath and the writing of this book. Thank you, Janis, for doing enthusiastically whatever I asked of you; I know a lot of what you did was not much fun, but contributed enormously.

My wife, Ellen, has given up a lot of me, without complaint—first during my pursuit of a victory for my clients in the Hadley case, and then during the writing of this book. Thank you, Ellen. I love and appreciate you.

Together:

We are forever grateful to our editor, Lori Zue, who turned our manuscript into a cherished legacy; publisher Sheryn Hara of Book Publishers Network, who saw great potential in our story; cover designer Laura Zugzda, who visually expressed our front cover concept; and graphics layout specialist, Stephanie Martindale, who had the difficult job of ensuring that all pieces, including photos, were placed in correct order.

We couldn't have asked for a more encouraging and supportive team to make our story come alive.

About the Authors

Suzanne G. Beyer

Suzanne G. Beyer, a Staten Island, New York native and graduate of the University of Vermont, majored in German with a minor in French. Although she still loves international languages, her love of writing (in English!) emerged above all.

Suzanne serves as associate editor and writer for Seattle's magazine, *Northwest Prime Time,* and also writes the monthly "Around Town" column for her local *Bothell-Kenmore Reporter* newspaper. Her many articles have appeared in twenty national magazines on a wide range of topics from health concerns to sports.

Her long-standing mantra was "I'll never write a book." Obviously, best-laid plans can change, and this book is proof of that!

Suzanne and her husband, Don, a retired fisheries scientist, live in Bothell, Washington. They have two grown daughters, Sabrina and Kalisa.

⚖ John S. Pfarr

A native of the Midwest with a bachelor of arts from Harvard University and his juris doctor from the University of Michigan Law School, John sees his primary role in his estate planning practice as that of educator. To this end, he is a co-author of four published books, in language understandable to his clients, on specific areas of estate planning. His office contains visual aids intended to take the mystique out of estate planning. He believes an educated client's active participation in the planning process produces an estate plan that captures the client's objectives as opposed to a plan where the lawyer simply tells the client what she or he needs.

The Inventor's Fortune is John's first published book-length story. In addition to making it fun and suspenseful, John uses the story as a vehicle to teach important aspects of the law.

John lives with his wife, Ellen, a social worker addressing the needs of abused and neglected children, in Essex, Connecticut. Between them, they have four children—Maria Berthoud, John Pfarr, Mary Ellen Robeson and Lauren Falzarano—and four grandchildren.